Your Personality Unlocked Living Life to Its Fullest

Anne Bulstrode, BBM FICB

Susan Geary, PhD.

Personality Dimensions is a Registered Trademark of
Career/LifeSkills Resources Inc.

Published by:
CLSR Inc.
Aurora, ON L4G 3V7
www.clsr.ca

Library and Archives Canada Cataloguing in Publication

Your personality unlocked: living life to its fullest / Anne
Bulstrode, BBM FICB, Susan Geary, PhD.

Bulstrode, Anne, 1961- author. | Geary, Susan Elizabeth,
1952- author.

Canadiana (print) 20210347244 | ISBN 9781894422598
(softcover)

LSH: Personality.

LCC BF698.B85 2021 | DDC 155.2—dc23:

CONTENTS

ACKNOWLEDGMENTS

First and foremost, we would like to thank CLSR for giving us permission to use the Personality Dimensions® terms, concepts, and ideas. We have especially appreciated Denise Hughes and Brad Whitehorn's support and encouragement through the long process of writing this book. We would also like to thank the other people that helped make this book a reality, those who read sections of the book and gave insightful feedback.

Families and friends always give so much support and make some sacrifices when authors are writing. Susan would like to thank her family for supporting her through this writing process. Specifically, she would like to thank John, Andrew, Jenn and especially her husband, Tim for supporting her through these times. She would like to dedicate this book to her beloved granddaughter in the hope that as she grows up, she might find this material helpful from time to time.

Susan would also like to thank her co-author, Anne Bulstrode. She would like to thank Anne for her intellectual honesty, her integrity and her desire to create a great end product.

Anne would like to thank her many friends and family that have supported her, asked questions about the book and how it is going and at times kept her motivated to keep on writing. Because they believe in what she is doing, and the difference Personality Dimensions® has made in both their business and personal lives. She would like to dedicate this book to 3 very special friends who have taken care of her and kept her sane through some very interesting times, Amy Layton, Diane Mitchell and Mia Ferrara. You are all such an important part of my life and I feel honoured to call you my friends.

Anne would also like to thank her co-author and wonderful writing partner Susan Geary. For her patience, her willingness to debate - when we don't agree, but we always come to a mutually agreeable solution, the way she embraces Personality Dimensions® and her ongoing support to create the best products we can in all that we write.

Last, but certainly not least, we would like to thank all of our workshop participants over the years who gave us invaluable insight into the dimensions from both an Introverted and Extraverted viewpoint and who were a driving force behind us writing this book.

.

1

Introduction to your Personality Dimensions

What does it mean to unlock your personality? It is all about understanding who you are. Why do you do things a certain way? Why do some things come so naturally for some, yet for others they can be a struggle? Why do we get along well with some people, but not others? It all comes down to our personalities. Identifying our personalities in four different ways, or dimensions, dates back to ancient times with a lot of stops along the way. Knowing who you are, who you REALLY are, and having a clear understanding of others and how they tick is something we can all benefit from.

As you read through the chapters in this book, you will start to have a much better understanding of who you are and the differences between you and other people. Once you get where they're coming from, and what is going on in their minds, you will find that you are seeing them in a different way; a way that will help you build and strengthen the way you interact with the people in your life.

Understanding your personality dimensions creates an experience that challenges you to know yourself better and to view people differently.

1

So, let's begin this journey of understanding by exploring who you are.

Completing the Questionnaire

If you're asked to describe yourself, we have no doubt you'd be able to tell us your likes and dislikes. But there is so much more to you that you may never have thought about.

That's where your dimensions come in. It's not HOW you are in a specific situation, but WHO you are on a day-to-day basis, that determines your dimensions. Your reactions and feelings out in the world are constantly impacted by other people and the situations you find yourself in. By understanding your dimensions, you will be able to react and manage the impact of those people and things in your day-to-day life.

No book could replace the value of working with a qualified professional to empower you to understand your actions and behaviours or provide you with feedback to help manage life. The goal with this questionnaire is to allow you to begin the self-reflection process.

You are born with your preferred dimensions and they develop over time. The people around you and the situations you experience affect who you are. As you get older, you learn how to use and develop the other aspects your personality.

Before you take the questionnaire, try this out first: find a piece of paper and a pen. Using the hand you normally write with, write your name down. Now switch hands and do it again. Notice that you can still do it, but it's not as comfortable, but you can do it if you need to. The same goes for your dimensions; you can call on each of the four when you need to, but you'll always be most comfortable using your most preferred dimension. To get the most out of this this questionnaire, don't just think of who you are now. Think of yourself over your lifetime. What kind of child were you? Were you a rebellious teenager? A focused post-secondary student? Career driven the second you graduated? All of those things speak to who you really are.

In the next few pages, you'll be asked to respond to 10 questions. For each question, you will rate four statements based on the following ranking:

4 = most like you

3 = second most like you

2 = third most like you

1 = least like you

1. I value:
A. _____ Freedom
B. _____ Relationships
C. _____ Knowledge
D. _____ Duty

2. I am comfortable:
A. _____ Trouble shooting
B. _____ Coaching
C. _____ Critiquing
D. _____ Planning

3. I learn best when the environment is:

A. _____ Fun, practical, applied
B. _____ Safe, conceptual, harmonious
C. _____ Rational, analytical, critical
D. _____ Specific, structured, practical

4. In general, I am:

A. _____ Energetic, innovative, realistic
B. _____ Conceptual, enthusiastic, supportive
C. _____ Competent, ingenious, logical
D. _____ Organized, responsible, dependable

5. I become stressed when there is too much:

A. _____ Authority, boredom, lack of action
B. _____ Conflict, lack of authority, detail
C. _____ Injustice, incompetence, illogical thinking
D. _____ Disorder, change, procrastination

6. In relationships, I seek:

A. _____ Excitement, stimulation, playfulness
B. _____ Meaning, intimacy, connection
C. _____ Respect, intellectual stimulation, directness
D. _____ Loyalty, responsibility, integrity

7. I enjoy:

A. _____ Being active, applying my skills, having fun

B. _____ Meaningful relationships, gaining insight about myself, helping others

C. _____ Being innovative, being competent, having a logical discussion

D. _____ Being of service to others, being recognized for the work I do, finishing a task

8. In groups, I tend to be:

A. _____ Playful, energetic, creative

B. _____ Inspirational, harmonizing, cooperative

C. _____ Analytical, independent, constructive

D. _____ Organized, committed, dependable

9. I am challenged by:

A. _____ Taking direction, arbitrary boundaries, routine

B. _____ Criticism, having to conform, isolation

C. _____ Repetitive activities, lack of information, small talk

D. _____ Risk taking, chaos, lack of control

10. When dealing with change I:

A. _____ Adjust in the here and now as change happens

B. _____ Understand how people are reacting to change & ensure that their needs are taken into account

C. _____ Think strategically and make systematic changes to achieve the vision

D. _____ Ensure that change happens effectively by implementing the specifics of the change plan

Scoring:

1. For each question that you complete, transfer the numbers you wrote next to A,B,C, & D in the appropriate space below

2. Then add the scores for column A, B, C and D and write the total in the space at the bottom

Question Number	A	B	C	D
Sample	4	2	1	3
1				
2				
3				
4				
5				
6				
7				
8				
9				
10				
Total				

If your highest score was A it is likely that you are, for the most part a Resourceful Orange.

If your highest score was B it is likely that you are, for the most part an Authentic Blue.

If your highest score was C it is likely that you are, for the most part an Inquiring Green.

If your highest score was D it is likely that you are, for the most part an Organized Gold.

The Four Dimensions

The following chart will give you a quick look at each of the four dimensions. In the rest of this book, you will see detailed descriptions of each. When you read the more detailed description you may find that you have a different preferred dimensions than you initially thought. But that's okay. The questionnaire isn't an exact science; it starts you down the path to discovering more about yourself.

Inquiring Green	• Needs: knowledge and competence • Uses logic when reasoning • Wants to have a rationale for everything • Focus is on patterns and systems • Objective and theoretical • Develops and applies strategies • Tends to be analytical, sceptical and critiquing • Tends to be a skilled long-range planner; contributing strategy, design & invention
Resourceful Orange	• Needs: freedom to act and make an impact • Has a matter-of-fact perspective • Gets bored quickly • Considers immediately needed actions when deciding • Focus is on creativity and skillfully doing • Gifted at deciding the best move to make in the moment • Able to adapt and improvise • Tends to be natural negotiators

Organized Gold	• Needs: belonging and being responsible • Believes in contribution to society and providing a service • Values the presence of order, lawfulness, security, institutions • Considers traditions and economic impact when deciding • Focus is on planning, security and stability • Develops and use rules for efficiency • Tends to be sequential and orderly • Appreciates family & cultural traditions
Authentic Blue	• Needs: personal growth and relationships • Likes to develop a unique identity • Uses values such as impact on people and unity when making decisions • Effective communicator • Develops and nurtures empathic relationships • Comes into a situation with an immediate impression of what is going on with people • Tends to see the big picture • Focus is on human potential

We Are All Plaid!

After completing the questionnaire and seeing some traits and characteristics of the four dimensions, you should now have a sense of which one(s) describe you best. However, keep in mind that no one is just one dimension. You will have one that will always be your go-to, but with parts of others woven in to make a plaid. Just like plaid, your personality is made up of mostly one colour or dimension, sometimes with a close secondary dimension, but has others running throughout – in different directions, with different amounts, in different intensities to create a unique pattern.

It's important to note that Personality Dimensions® can't and doesn't explain all human behaviour. You are not limited to being a certain way or experiencing certain things because of your preferred dimension. Quite the opposite, in fact! By understanding yourself better you will be BETTER able to adapt to the situation and experience things differently. With practice, you can even get better at writing your name with your opposite hand. Most of all remember that no dimension is better than another, each has its own unique talents and behaviours.

2

Where do you get your energy?

Knowing your dimensions is the first step on the path to living your life to its fullest. The next step is understanding where you get your energy from and how you can recharge it; also known as Introversion and Extraversion.

Being Introverted or Extraverted doesn't speak to how shy or outgoing you are, it's all about where your energy comes from. Extraverts get their energy from the outside world. They recharge their batteries by being around people and interacting with them, and they direct their energy outwards in the form of action. They are the conversation starters and the socializers. Introverts, on the other hand, tend to get their energy from within. They need time alone to recharge their batteries and direct their energy inwards in the form of reflection. They are the listeners and observers.

Keep in mind that you aren't completely Introverted or completely Extraverted. In fact, Carl Jung - the first person to write about this - once said, "There is no such thing as a pure Introvert or Extrovert." Introversion and Extraversion is a scale with two ends; and you will find yourself somewhere between the two of them.

Introversion is not measured in levels of shyness. Because

someone is an Introvert doesn't mean that they are shy. Introverts can be very warm and outgoing people, and great at interacting with others. At the same time, not all Extraverts are outgoing and sociable; they, too, can be shy when meeting others for the first time.

To show how Introverts and Extraverts act differently, consider how each one prepares for a presentation. Preparing for a presentation means you need to spend time gathering and organizing information on your own. For an Extravert this stage can be exhausting. After a day alone, an Extravert may need to find someone to speak with to get their energy back. For the Introvert, however, this part of the process is energizing. It gives them the time they need to think and reflect without interruptions from others, which is how they work best.

When it comes to the actual presentation, the opposite is true. The Extraverts are in their element. They find presenting to the audience and interacting with them very energizing. Introverts, however, find this part of the process draining. Introverts need some quiet time alone after the presentation to re-energize. Extraverts and Introverts can be good at doing both the preparation and the presentation. What's different is how they prepare, and what they have to do to afterwards to regain their energy.

Introverts do their best decision-making, thinking and learning when they have the time for quiet reflection and are able to work on their own. Extraverts are at their best when they can interact with others, discuss their thoughts, and brainstorm new and creative ideas. Introverts may actually find that the standard brainstorming process shuts down their creative juices. It doesn't allow them the time they need to process ideas before building on them or reacting to them.

When Extraverts are thinking, they process their thoughts out loud. Introverts tend to do all of their thought-processing internally. This can be frustrating for both Extraverts and Introverts when they are working together. Extraverts can feel like Introverts are not contributing to the process because they are not saying a lot. What they may not realize is that Introverts need time to process and will add their ideas once they have had the chance to think them through fully. Introverts may feel they can't get a word in edgewise or that they aren't being heard when they speak up. This can be frustrating for them as they never know if the Extravert is planning to do what they say, or just throwing out ideas. If Introverts and Extraverts don't understand each other, this can lead to major communication problems.

Understanding the difference between Introversion and Extraversion will help you better deal with each of the different dimensions. The first step in understanding the difference is to find out whether you are an Introvert or an Extravert. You may think you know who you are but take a couple of minutes to complete the simple Introversion/Extraversion questionnaire that follows. You might be surprised to discover you're not who you think you are. Or, at the very least, not who society has convinced you that you are.

1.   A.   I am energized by being with others
      B.   I am energized by time alone

2.   A.   I tend to think out loud
      B.   I tend to think inside my head

3. A. I share my thoughts and feelings

   B. I tend to think inside my head

4. A. I tend to act first and then think

   B. I keep my thoughts and feelings to myself

5. A. I prefer problem solving by talking it through with others

   B. I prefer problem solving by working it through on my own

6. A. Others see me as outgoing

   B. Others see me as quiet

7. A. I have a broad circle of friends

   B. I have an intimate circle of friends

8. A. After a day working with others, I am energized

   B. After a day working on my own, I am energized

9. A. I prefer to have a lot of interests

   B. I prefer to have a few interests in depth

10. A. I tend to show a sense of enthusiasm and energy

    B. I tend to show a sense of calmness

Total number of As _____

Total number of B's _____

If you have more As than Bs you are more Extraverted.

If you have more Bs than As you are more Introverted.

Just like the questionnaire you took in the first chapter, this one isn't an exact science. It doesn't tell you how Introverted or Extraverted you are, even if you answered with all As or all Bs. However, it helps you get a better understanding of where you get your energy from, and how you recharge your batteries.

Joys of being an Extravert

There are many great things about being an Extravert! Because you get your energy from the external world, you thrive when you are involved in activities and/or social situations. Involvement in a bunch of activities like work, sports, family time, social functions and volunteer work are energizing for you. Social functions, like parties, family get-togethers or work meetings will more often energize you rather than drain your energy. You can enjoy yourself even with people that you don't know. However, Extraverts still need some downtime to avoid getting burned out; just not as much as Introverts.

As an Extravert you like sharing your thoughts and feelings, brainstorming, and problem solving with others. You excel in family or work situations where you can be collaborative and build on each other's ideas to create solutions. Like patting your head while rubbing your belly, you have the benefit of being able to think and talk at the same time. So, when asked a question, you can just start talking and formulating your message in the moment.

Others are likely to know what you are thinking or feeling because you freely share what's going on in your mind – even when your thoughts are half formed. This helps you to influence others because you can talk through things and shape decisions. You tend to act first and then think. While this helps you to get your points across and react quickly, your quick reaction may cause you to reach a conclusion that needs more thought before it can be put into action.

You prefer to problem solve by talking things through with others. You like bouncing your ideas off of other people and listening to their thoughts. In an environment where collaboration and teamwork are encouraged, you thrive.

When it comes to your social life, you tend to like having a large circle of friends. You don't need to have a deep, meaningful conversation with others to feel they are your friends. You are happy to just hang out with your buddies and enjoy some light banter. Sometimes just going to a shopping mall or festival, or any place where there are lots of people, can be energizing. You usually don't mind networking and may even enjoy it, because you are comfortable introducing yourself to strangers and engaging in conversation.

You enjoy a wide range of interests, and can talk about many different things. You may have lots of hobbies and interests and don't feel the need to be an expert in any of them in order to engage with others. Even a slight interest in something can be enough for you to enjoy having a conversation with another person. After a day spent with others or doing different activities, you feel energized. For you, a good day is one where there are many interactions and a variety of different activities.

Your energy can also be very engaging to others. You are comfortable being the life of the party; happy to socialize with different people and talk about almost any topic. If you're not interested in something, you'll happily contribute to a conversation on the topic just to be part of the conversation. Extraverts are engagers and thrive in the company of a wide variety of people and across multiple interests.

Challenges of being an Extravert

It might seem like Extraverts are THE person to aim to be. You are outgoing. You are a great communicator. You can make decisions and act quickly when you need to. Who wouldn't want to be an Extravert? Here's the truth. Being an Extravert does not make you likable, or effective, in social and professional situations. Nor does it make you a happier or more effective human being.

You don't like long stretches of alone time and you also don't like analyzing situations and finding solutions on your own. You tend to feel bored, lonely and emotionally fatigued if left to yourself for too long. The best way for you to manage alone time is to plan breaks where you will be able to see others and interact with them in the real world.

Because you tend to act first and think later, you sometimes give the wrong impression, especially to people who you don't know very well. Some Extraverts just don't have a mute button - let alone autocorrect - so as an Extravert, you might make comments that annoy or upset other people. When you are in a sensitive communication situation, you need to actively work to pause and think about what you are about to say, before blurting out the first thought that comes to your mind. You are at a much greater risk of saying things you can't take back and that you regret.

To say it's helpful to actively contribute to a conversation is one thing; but a room full of Extraverts talking through a problem, may not result in the discovery of the best solution. You can have such a good time brainstorming problems and solutions with others that you may forget to ask what the quieter Introverts think. So, while Introverts are thinking things through before sharing their ideas, Extraverts can plough ahead as if the Introverts are not even there. Everyone is more likely to miss out on the thoughtful analysis that Introverts bring to the table. You need to actively find ways to include Introverts in the conversation.

You are generally outgoing. You are often drawn to other outgoing people because you share the same kind of energy. However, you may misinterpret the quieter Introverts as being cool or disinterested and not take the time to get to know them. In this way, you miss out on benefiting from the rich thinking that occurs inside an Introvert's head. You need to understand that although Introverts may seem calm and quiet, and maybe even disinterested, they really have lots to share if you give them the space to think, and time to speak.

Although you enjoy having a big circle of friends, you may not develop the same level of closeness that Introverts have with their friends. You may have a lot of people who you can technically turn to, but you may not have anyone who you would feel comfortable confiding in about more personal or sensitive issues. You may find it helpful to develop deeper relationships with one or two people that you can confide in and turn to for mutual support.

Extraverts tend to have a wide range of interests but are less likely to get fully involved in one. To overcome a lack of in-depth knowledge on any one subject, Extraverts often rely on others to contribute their thoughts, expertise, and insight or become a subject matter expert on important topics.

Some people can find your sense of enthusiasm and energy off-putting. Introverts especially, may think you are 'too much' in addition to being energy drainers. In order to deal with you, Introverts are more likely to shut down rather than build up the energy to interact with you. Be aware of your potential impact on Introverts, and where it is important, tone down your enthusiasm so that everyone stays in the conversation.

Joys of being an Introvert

You enjoy having time to think things through before making a decision or sharing your decision with others. You like being able to mull over ideas in your head before presenting them. A well thought out idea is much better than one that is off-the-cuff. You often have the same conversation that Extraverts have when thinking things through, yours is just done as a conversation in your head. You get joy out of arriving at a well thought out plan, and sound decision-making gives you confidence.

You need time alone to recharge your batteries. This can be an advantage because you don't need to have others around you all the time. You enjoy solitary time. You are not dependent on other people for your energy. You will often thrive in situations where you can spend time alone reading a book, going for a walk or enjoying nature. If it is not possible to be alone, you prefer to meet with just one or two people at a time. This is much less draining than having to deal with a large group of people. You are far more likely to want to have a coffee with a couple of friends than a get together with a larger group for an outing.

You are often very private when it comes to sharing your thoughts and feelings. There needs to be a level of trust and comfort before you will share them. Once you do let another person into your life, you will share your thoughts and feelings in a genuine way. This allows you to enjoy much more meaningful relationships.

Being quiet can be an advantage. Often you are quiet because you are listening and observing the world around you. You enjoy having the time to take everything in and reflect on it.

The fact that you prefer a smaller, close circle of friends means that you really get to know them. It can take a while to get to know you as you don't tend to share your thoughts and feelings openly with everyone. However, once others really get to know you, chances are your friendship will be deep, meaningful, and long lasting.

Challenges of being an Introvert

It might sound like Introverts are THE person to be. You are a great listener. You have memorable one-on-one conversations. You take your time to think before you speak and give thoughtful answers. Who wouldn't want to be an Introvert? The truth though, is that being an Introvert doesn't naturally make you tranquil or an effective problem solver. Nor does it make you a happier or more effective person.

Your need for time alone can be challenging, especially if you work in a fast-paced environment that demands speed and efficiency. You often feel like you don't get enough time to be alone. Most of us have many demands on our time. Your days are often spent with other people whether it is at work, in meetings and working with others, or at home with family and friends. To overcome this you can try to schedule alone time. This may not be possible at work but at home you need to find a way to do it.

You are often misunderstood, especially by people who are very Extraverted, as being uninterested and unengaged. In order to push against this stereotype, you have to actively try to make yourself visible, noticed and heard when you are thinking through your answers and contributions. By keeping your thoughts to yourself you can come off as being standoffish. Really, you just need to think things through before you share and meaningfully engage. It is in your best interest to actively engage with people around you, even if it's outside your comfort zone.

You also can come off as indecisive, which can be frustrating for others. The fact is, you like to take more time when making decisions. You think them through and weigh the options in your head. By the time you make a decision, you're sure of it. You can also be seen as not wanting to participate in problem solving conversations, when really you are already doing just that - problem solving - in your head. Because of this barrier, you need to be vocal and upfront about your need to think things through before contributing ideas. Also, when a decision is not going to have any major impact, you need to learn to trust your gut and go with what feels right in the moment. This will show others that you can sometimes come to a decision quickly (it is only the major ones where you are more comfortable taking your time).

You can be seen as very calm. However, this can be interpreted as being unengaged or just plain not interested in the people or activities going on around you. This means that you need to make an extra effort to be seen as engaged in the conversation.

What Extraverts Can Do to Engage Introverts

Remember that Introverts come across as being calm and/or quiet. Don't be put off by this. Take the time to get to know them. As their comfort level increases, they will be much more likely to chat and share with you.

Don't assume that if an Introvert is quiet it is because they don't have anything to say or that they are consciously withholding information or ideas. It isn't because they don't want to talk to you. They like to think things through before they share. It could also be that you have not given them enough space to get into the conversation.

In order to be an effective listener, you need to learn to take time to pause, and give the Introvert an opportunity to think through what they want to say, then allow them to say it, without being interrupted. This can be challenging for you, but it's important that you work hard to avoid the temptation of filling silence with more chatter. Sometimes it's as simple as developing the technique of pouring another cup of coffee. This simple act breaks the conversation flow and allows others to think before speaking.

You need to take the time to ask what the Introvert thinks about a topic. It doesn't need to be like pulling teeth. They have ideas they want to share, but they need to be given enough time to think them through so that they will be clear and insightful.

If you want to bring out the best in an Introvert, give them a heads-up to let them know what you want to talk about and what your hopes and expectations are for the conversation. This will give them time to think through what they want to say when you get together.

It is also useful to know that Introverts may prefer email or texting because they can take the time to formulate and review their ideas. They can't edit their words once they leave their mouth but typing gives them the option to revise and refine their thoughts. It takes far less energy, if you're an Introvert, to communicate via written messages.

What Introverts Can Do to Engage Extraverts

It is no easy task for you to engage Extraverts. It can be downright intimidating. However, it is important for you to speak up and be heard. Introverts often say, "It is as if I am invisible. I can say something, get no reaction and then someone else says the same or something similar five minutes later and it is hailed as a great idea." You need to find ways to engage the Extraverts and be noticed. You don't have to be someone you aren't, but you do need to make sure you are an active participant, and a solid contributor to the conversation. If you feel ignored the first time, you need to do your best to try a second time to be heard. Sometimes the same idea will have more impact when it is repeated. Making eye contact with the speakers will let them know that you are interested in what they have to say and encourage them to include you in a conversation.

Remember that Extraverts like to think out loud, but it doesn't mean that their ideas are solid, well thought out, or complete. Extraverts are most comfortable talking things out with other people contributing ideas. An idea is not a solution. It is a recommendation only. Extraverts expect ideas to be changed as thoughts are discussed and honed by other peoples' input. You may find this frustrating because usually, when you express an idea it has been well thought out. To overcome this, you sometimes need to share your ideas in the early stages of the conversation and not wait until you have thought them through.

If you feel you need time to think things through you should tell the Extraverts, so that they don't think you are disinterested. There is nothing wrong with asking for a moment or a longer stretch of time to carefully consider and formulate your ideas. You should not be afraid to explain that you just need some time to consider all the information and/or options – be it at work or when deciding where to have dinner.

If you aren't ready to contribute, why not ask a question or two? Information gathering is a great way to be part of the conversation. And it buys you some time before you express your ideas.

Even though you may prefer to communicate in writing, Extraverts tend to like to talk either in person or on the phone. At times a phone or in person conversation may help you sort things out more quickly.

Introverts or Extraverts, both have great qualities. It does not matter which of these you are. What really matters is that you embrace your joys, work to overcome your challenges and engage others in a meaningful way that works for both of you.

3

Life Values

Your needs and values influence every aspect of your life –
how you are as a partner, friend, or parent; the people you are
drawn to and what you decide to do with your life. Your core
needs are key to who you are, and you will do everything
consciously and unconsciously to have your needs met. When
they have been met you function better as a human. You feel
confident. You feel inspired. You feel in-tune with yourself.
That said, when your needs are not met, you lose that drive,
and that interest. You no longer feel energized. Instead you
feel tired and down. Work can take effort. Your values are
what is important to you and they guide you to act in ways that
feel comfortable and consistent with who you are.

Every dimension has its own unique needs and values. To
really understand the difference between each of the
dimensions, you must first look at how their needs and values
are different. In chapter one, you did some work to figure out
what your dimensions are. Now you'll dive deeper into what
your dimensions say about your needs and values. Pay close
attention to your preferred dimensions first, then take a look
at which others make up your plaid.

Inquiring Green

 As an Inquiring Green you need to feel competent and to be seen that way by others. When learning something new, you will gather as much information as possible so that you can act competently. For example, an Inquiring Green dog owner will buy all the videos, how-to books, and take a class, so that they can feel as informed as they can be. If you feel incompetent or if others call you incompetent, you can get offended, or your confidence can get shaken. You also have little patience for other people's incompetence. You would rather work alone than be stuck working with someone who is incompetent.

What also sets you apart from the other dimensions is your ongoing thirst-and-search for knowledge. As an Inquiring Green parent, you don't just read one book on sleep training, you read five. You read blogs and articles about the pros and cons of each method. You might even read studies on long term effects of sleep training. You want all the knowledge possible and will not rely on one or two sources as being enough. You strive to get facts and data about the way things work as opposed to the way people work. You have a lifelong curiosity and need to gain knowledge.

From an early age you have often asked why – "why is the sky blue?" or "why does it snow?" As a child you may have looked at a toy, taken it apart, and then tried to put it back together again, even if wasn't the kind of toy that was supposed to be taken apart.

Over time, as an Inquiring Green, you develop values that will help you achieve your basic needs. You are a thinker. You prize logical and rational thinking and pride yourself on this. You enjoy listening to new ideas and are happy to explore them, as long as they make sense. If an idea is not logical, you might want to challenge it, or stop listening. As an Inquiring Green, you might just tune out ideas that you think are not good enough.

You are an independent thinker and place a high value on achievement and intelligence. You strive to achieve whatever goals you set. Your chosen career often becomes a place where you can achieve results and you can work hard to be successful. As an independent thinker, you don't want others telling you what to do, how to think, or which career to pursue. You tend to be drawn to friends who stimulate you intellectually.

Inquiring Greens are known to value scientific inquiry. You like to find out why things are the way they are in nature and science and why they work the way they do. As a child, you may have enjoyed math, physics and chemistry because you liked the logical reasoning and universal laws behind these topics.

You value progress and improvement. You don't tend to dwell on the past or present; instead you focus on the future and the opportunities to do more and to do better.

You like to use your knowledge to make improvements. You are the type of person who recommends and applies effort to change how things are done. However, this can cause conflict or misunderstanding with others because you have a tendency to not be tactful when implementing change. Remember, you may think it's logical and forward thinking to pursue change, but others may not see it this way, which leads to possible struggles with people - and scenarios - that work against progress.

Resourceful Orange

 As a Resourceful Orange you value freedom. You want the freedom to make your own choices about how you live your life. You want to be able to express yourself in whatever way you choose – whether in the arts, music, business or adventure. You don't want to be micromanaged in any aspect of your life. Without this kind of freedom, you can feel constrained and boxed in. If you get your back up you could act out. As a parent, you like to give your children lots of freedom because you value it yourself. You enjoy relationships with partners where there is enough room for you to each live your lives without feeling constrained.

You love excitement and new things. As a child you used your imagination to create games and activities. You were always looking for something exciting to do, which wasn't the best thing when you were supposed to be sitting quietly and respectfully in a classroom! You like to live in your five senses - sight, sound, touch, taste and smell - as much as possible and have new sensations and experiences. You love to be spontaneous and go with your feelings because that is when you feel most alive.

You thrive on variety and love change in your life. You probably won't live in the same house that was your childhood home or go back to the same place you went to on your last vacation. Being bored, and doing the same things day-after-day are hard for you, so you make decisions and live your life with variety in mind.

You take pride in getting good at and wowing others with what you do, whether it's music, acting, arts and crafts, sports, cooking, business or politics. You aim to be the best and you have no problem practicing in front of others as you perfect your skills. You love the immediate rush you get when others recognize all the hard work you invest into a project or a great performance.

You want to make your mark by standing out from the crowd. Because of your drive to make an impact, you thrive in using your creativity, flexibility, and talent to perform under pressure to achieve results.

Not surprisingly, you enjoy taking risks and testing limits. Sometimes, you will do something just to prove you can - not just to prove it to others but more importantly to prove it to yourself. You don't like easy tasks, as they quickly bore you. A challenge gets your adrenalin going and keeps you on your toes. Quite frequently, work or sports that require you to take physical risks such as off-shore oil drilling, high rise construction, mountain climbing, sky diving, surfing or white-water rafting appeals to the younger version of you.

You believe in taking the time to enjoy yourself and have a good time. You are spontaneous, fun loving and go-with-the-flow. Your goal is to impress and entertain. Your motto is "seize the day" - life is to be enjoyed.

Organized Gold

As an Organized Gold you get self-worth through duty and responsibility. Much of what you do is directed at enhancing your sense of belonging. Family is so important that you often believe that looking after them is the most important thing that you do. You spend time and energy providing a stable home for your family and ensuring that everything runs smoothly so that family members can flourish. You sacrifice and love fiercely, often putting the needs of your loved ones ahead of yourself. Your self-worth is heavily tied to the happiness of the closest people in your life. At work and in the community, you like to be a member of different groups because it helps you provide security and support for others as well as feeling needed. At work, you join committees, sports teams, social clubs, or charitable groups. In the community, you are an active member of the groups that you value and feel obligated to support. As a parent, you are often the person involved in the Parent Teacher Association and also the one who volunteers at school dances and on pizza days. You happily coach your kids' sports teams or are the proud dance mom and/or dad, helping your children prepare for competitions. You are extremely loyal to your friends and to the important people in your life. Because a sense of belonging is so important, you can suffer if you feel left behind.

More than any of the other dimensions, you need to feel a sense of security. You understand that life is unpredictable and even if things are going great, they can easily take a turn for the worst. Knowing how easily a health or financial crisis may occur - such as a car accident or job layoff - you take on the role of safety and security protector for yourself and others. You work hard to ensure things go as planned. You also are the one who others can trust to have a contingency plan in place, just in case. You are also likely to have insurance as a way to safeguard against life's disasters. Your motto in life is "be prepared."

You like order and structure and believe in the importance of a pecking order. You like making lists to help stay organized and on track, then checking things off as you complete them. Your view is that once you've received your marching orders there should be a chain of command where everyone has clearly defined roles and responsibilities. You often admire institutions such as the monarchy, church, or military because of the traditional ways they have flourished through the generations. You often aspire to leadership positions yourself and can be an effective leader in your community, politics, education, and business. If you decide to become part of a volunteer organization, you may want to take on leadership responsibilities to help ensure that things are done right.

Organized Golds embrace duty and responsibility, believing that if everyone contributes their fair share, the world will be a better place. That's why you take responsibility for your family, work, and community very seriously. Once you say you will do something you always do your best to get it done. You believe you need to work first and play later. You need positive recognition and work tirelessly for others in the hope that they will appreciate what you do. You often end up doing tasks that others don't want to do, such as taking out the garbage, paying the bills, or getting the car serviced. That said, you won't be smiling while you are dragging the stinky bag to the curb. You'll do it, but you may feel resentful if no one acknowledges what you have done. You don't want to be taken for granted. You need the recognition you deserve.

Authentic Blue

As an Authentic Blue one of your major driving forces is self-actualization. You want to be the best possible version of yourself that you can be. You are always trying to improve yourself, whether that means taking a class, reading or talking with others. Finding meaning and significance in your life is an ongoing journey. As a parent, you will read books, attend parenting workshops and reflect on your own experiences so that you can improve your parenting skills. In other significant relationships you will also focus on how you can learn and grow so that those relationships can be more meaningful.

Over time, you have developed a set of values that help you to achieve your needs. With a strong belief in human potential, you tend to want to help others grow and develop. You are more likely to choose professions such as teaching or counselling where you can contribute to society in a meaningful way. As a parent, it is important to you to nurture and bring out the best in your children.

You like to look for positive attributes in others. You're much more likely to put your faith in a person than to search for their faults. You are very forgiving and believe most people are inherently good. Sometimes, this can be seen as gullible, but by having this attitude toward others you are able to build relationships based on mutual trust and respect. You feel confidant when you are valued and given positive recognition for your efforts.

You are spiritual, however, that does not necessarily mean you are attracted to mainstream religions. You may be more attracted to alternative spiritual practices, such as meditation or yoga. Living a meaningful, ethical life that contributes to the greater good of humanity is important to you.

You see yourself as unique and like it when others recognize your individuality. Your unique identity may show itself in the clothes you wear, the lifestyle you choose, the way you furnish your home, or the way you interact with others.

Relationships are very important to you and you want them to be mutual, caring and nurturing. You only consider a person to be a friend once you truly get to know and trust each other – warts and all. If you are an Introvert this can take quite a bit of time. You don't like to live with conflict. You prefer to build bridges with and between others so that you can live a life that is full of harmony.

You are much more interested in collaboration and putting people in a room to discuss a topic or problem solve - especially if you are an Extravert. You like working with others because you believe that two heads are better than one. Your imagination helps you find innovative and resourceful ways to understand and solve problems.

You aim to be authentic and genuine in all that you do and expect others to do the same. You live by your values and strong code of ethics and usually won't go against them. If you have to go against your values it can be painful. You can get angry if you see other people acting in an unethical way. If you are an Introvert you are more likely to have an internal struggle with unethical behaviour, but if you are an Extravert you are more likely to actively protest it.

Understanding your own values, and realizing what is important to you, are key steps in being able to live your life to its fullest. But it's not enough to know only about yourself, since there are other people in your life who have values and priorities that are different from yours; it's equally as important to understand what makes them tick.

Communication is key; and you already know that everyone has different communication styles that they prefer using, not just at work, but in every aspect of life. As you read through the next chapter, ask yourself if you are comfortable with each of the dimensions' individual communication styles. Can you see why you identify with some and not others? If you needed to, can you use the other styles?

4

In Communications

How you communicate with others, and how you want others to communicate with you can be a tricky balance. Understanding this makes things a lot easier for everyone involved. Remember your plaid? Even if you only have a small stripe of another colour running through yours, you can still use it to build your communication skills and understanding of others. Your unique plaid also means that you might just like communicating slightly differently from someone that shares your preferred dimension.

As you read through this chapter, take note of the communication styles that you are comfortable with that are not your preferred dimension. Also think about the people you regularly communicate with and how you can make a few changes to your approach.

Inquiring Green

How Inquiring Greens Communicate

You have a very direct and to the point communication style; you aren't a fan of small talk at all. You prefer to sit down and get right to work.

You are all about getting to the facts, and not as much into the outwardly emotional side of things. When your own emotions come into play, you can really struggle and may need to take a breather before coming back to the table. You will find it equally difficult to deal with other people's emotional responses.

What are Inquiring Green Communication Strengths?

You are good at being cool under pressure. Other dimensions can see this as being standoffish or insensitive, but that is not your intention. You just don't wear your heart on your sleeve.

You are very good at presenting the big picture in a logical, concise way. You like using diagrams, pictures, or models to explain a process.

You prefer to only share your ideas with others if you are comfortable with them and know the subject you are talking about. You're not big on winging it or faking it. It is important to you to be seen as competent. When you talk about something, you have done your research. You know what you're talking about. Once you have told others something, you don't like having to say it again.

The Best Ways to Communicate with Inquiring Greens

You enjoy a good debate with people whose opinion you respect. If the discussion is with someone you don't respect or the topic isn't interesting to you, you can tune out. You are not interested in small talk just for the sake of it. The topic needs to be interesting to you otherwise you might see it as unimportant.

You prefer to leave emotions out of the conversation and to stick to the facts, ideas and theories. When communicating with you, others should know what they're talking about and not pretend to know things they don't. You will see right through them.

You want a clear understanding of overall expectations so that you have a good idea of the situation and can effectively work towards what is expected. You like it when others start with the big picture and use diagrams and models as a way of explaining their ideas.

Resourceful Orange

How Resourceful Oranges Communicate

You like to express your ideas and make decisions quickly, and move on to the next thing. Other dimensions can see this as being hasty or unfeeling; that's not the case, you just want to keep going.

You use down to earth language when communicating. You don't like or see the need for long discussions, especially about the meanings of words or abstract ideas, and you like to use action orientated language.

When presenting verbal instructions, you prefer to be very open-ended and give few of them. You like to do things your own way and assume others feel the same. However, you are always willing to give more detailed instructions when asked.

What are Resourceful Orange Communication Strengths?

You are charismatic, enthusiastic and can be pretty persuasive when you want to be. You are a good listener for shorter periods of time. Your ability to know what people want, your sense of fairness and eye for opportunity make you good at negotiations.

When you give instructions, or are recounting a story, you get straight to the point. You are happy to give more details if you're asked for them. You don't mince words and like to say what you mean from the get go. You like to choose your own way of doing things, and want to give others the same freedom.

The Best Ways to Communicate with Resourceful Oranges

You like communications to be short and to the point. You get frustrated when conversations get long and drawn out. You also aren't a big fan of abstract ideas or long discussions about little details. You respond best to language that is light and upbeat and would prefer a demonstration rather than an explanation. You love action and appreciate it when others make it fun to communicate with you.

Freedom is super important to you. You need to be able to express your own ideas and do things your own way. You don't like being told how something is supposed to be done. You are able to make decisions quickly. Once you've been given information, you want to weigh in right away.

Organized Gold

How Organized Golds Communicate

You are very clear and precise when communicating with others. You give instructions in a logical step-by-step manner, making sure you include all of the necessary details. A sense of belonging is very important to you and you want to work with others to ensure that your communications are fully understood. You are always willing to respond to questions and help clarify things.

The past and traditions are very important to you, so you tend to use traditional language and draw on past experience when giving examples.

What are Organized Gold Communication Strengths?

You are very dependable and reliable. If you tell another person you will do something, it will get done, done right, and done on time.

Structure and process are often important to you and you tend to present information in an organized, step-by-step way.

You are excellent at keeping your conversations from getting sidetracked. If you see a conversation starting to drift in the wrong direction, you will bring everyone back on track, in a well-mannered and appropriate way.

The Best Ways to Communicate with Organized Golds

You like communications to be well structured and thought out. When a task is being explained to you, it is important to be clear about what the task is, how it should be done and what the deadline is.

When it comes to theory or abstract ideas, you need to have a thorough understanding of how practical it is and what exactly it will be used for. You need to be able to ask questions to fully understand it.

You like to focus on the past and the present. When others use examples to make points, it is important they use past examples and show how they will work in the current situation. You like specific examples and real, non-jargon words.

Authentic Blue

How Authentic Blues Communicate

You communicate well both in writing and verbally. You are expressive and when an issue really matters, you can be very convincing. You often speak passionately and enthusiastically. Giving and receiving positive feedback builds your confidence.

As a gifted storyteller you like to use metaphors, analogies and personal experiences to get your point across. You like to present big picture ideas first before getting into the details. You can take a while to make a point because it is important that you consider the feelings of others and that everyone understands what you are saying. You are good at reading other people's emotions and can adjust your style when need be.

What are Authentic Blue Communication Strengths?

You are a good listener. You are intuitive, so are able to hear what is, and what isn't, being said. You instinctively know what the other person really means, not just what they are saying. This allows you to get to the heart of the matter. You use personal examples to make a point. You do this because it allows you to connect with others on a deeper level.

Reading body language is also your strength; you are able to pick up on hidden cues and resolve misunderstandings before they happen.

The Best Ways to Communicate with Authentic Blues

You like others to use analogies and personal stories when communicating with you. You like to feel a connection to others and this way of explaining points makes it feel more real for you.

You are a big picture thinker, so others should always start off with the big picture and work towards the details. They should use universal language and concepts.

Self-actualization is very important to you and you are always looking for ways to make things better for yourself and others. When communicating with you, it is important others focus on the future and possibilities. You like it when people explain how their approach will positively impact others and fit into your values.

For the most part, people don't communicate in a way that is hard for you on purpose; it's just what's natural for them. Reading about different communication styles is easy, but truly understanding them, and being willing to adjust your approach can be difficult... But it is worth doing so you can live life to its fullest.

In the next chapter you'll get a sense of how the dimensions relate to each other, where you can run into trouble, and how to support each other.

5

In Relationships

We form many different types of relationships as we journey through life. Our family, friends, co-workers and members of the community all come in and out of our lives at different times and in different ways. Some of these relationships will be easy right from the start but often, they take work – a lot of work. It's hard to know for sure what determines our ability to get along better with one person over another, but differences in the dimensions may be one of the reasons why some relationships are harder than others.

In this chapter you will see how the differences in the four dimensions can impact relationships. When you read through this section, try to remember your plaid – You have one main colour, but stripes of others also run through it to create a unique pattern. Start by jumping into your most preferred dimension, and make your way through based on your plaid. See if you can identify the Personality Dimensions of the people you have close relationships with. Later, in Chapter 8, you will learn more about how to begin reading other people's dimensions, using your Personality Radar, so don't jump ahead just yet.

Inquiring Green

 You feel deeply but can have a hard time outwardly expressing your feelings. You are logical and objective, and very good at putting your emotions aside. Some of the other dimensions might see this as cold or unfeeling, but reality is that you care very much for, and are incredibly faithful to, the people who are close to you. You just aren't the kind of person who wears your heart on your sleeve. That's okay, because your calm and even-tempered presence can work to everyone's advantage in many situations; even creating a sense of balance with people who are the opposite.

You are very principled and need to be around people you respect. Like other areas of your life, you put high expectations on yourself and your relationships. You like a good debate; but you need to be careful to not come across as argumentative. You like to share common goals, but need some autonomy when putting them in place. If you're an Introvert, you'll need some alone time to stay energized while working on goals.

You don't like repetition or redundancy. If you have said "I love you" once, you are likely to think "why do I need to say it again?" From your point of view, the fact that you are still in the relationship and have stated your love for the other person means that there is no need to say it again. You believe that actions speak louder than words.

You aren't big on large displays of affection; they just don't come naturally to you. Feelings are important to you, but they aren't always the highest priority. You might not even remember to say thank you and don't always hold your partner's hand in public. That being said, when in private, you can be affectionate with those you are close to. As partners, you are strong, loving and courageous and put a lot of effort into your relationships.

You thrive at separating your relationships with different people. You can easily keep your work life and family life separate. A bad day at work doesn't necessarily translate to a stressful night at home with the family. You are very capable of leaving work at work.

You are independent, and you like to raise your children to be the same. You are also consistent in the way you relate to your children. For you, it is important to be fair in all of your relationships.

You are most comfortable being with people you respect and who respect you. You build relationships on a solid foundation of trust. However, if that trust is broken, they will have a hard time winning you back. You relate to people based on your expertise. You want to be in relationships with people who have interesting ideas and opinions that challenge you. Someone who won't engage in meaningful debate and discussion will frustrate you. You need and want to feel valued and understood.

Resourceful Orange

Your relationships are based on common interests. You have many interests so you will have a lot of friends to go with them. You tend to be very spontaneous, like to have fun and prefer to be with people who like the same things – friends who can pick up and go on a dime the next time something good comes up. Extraverted Resourceful Oranges get energized by being out with friends all day. Introverts still want to take part, but need time at the end of the day to recharge.

In relationships you want freedom and independence, where you can be yourself. You get stressed or angry if people try to control or change you, and this could be a real challenge in some relationships. This is especially true in a parent-child relationship where the child is a Resourceful Orange.

It is important for you to keep relationships exciting and interesting, for both you and your friends or with your partner. You are generous and enjoy doing things for other people. You love being surprised and even more, you love surprising others, whether it be with an actual gift or action. You have often made the gift yourself, so that it is unique and special for the recipient.

You go with the flow and are laidback and flexible. You are good at chilling out, taking a breather and compromising just to keep things moving. That's because you're pretty agreeable and because you can't be bothered with conflict. That's not to say you are a pushover. Not even close. In reality, you are quite competitive, and if you see conflict as a challenge you will try to win. Introverted Resourceful Oranges will internalize conflict more than Extraverts who want to deal with it right away. If you are watching a group of children play together, it'll often be the Resourceful Orange kids who are busting their butts to win.

You want your relationships to be easy, warm and playful and you may not last long in relationships where you aren't happy. You know what you need and if you're not getting it, you might decide to call it quits and move on. You tend to live in the here and now and you don't dwell on the past.

You put a high value on honesty and a sense of humor and if asked for your opinion, you won't hold back. You expect others to be honest, open and direct with you.

Organized Gold

 You need to feel a sense of belonging and are the type of person who wants, needs and works toward the security of being in a committed relationship. If you don't feel your partner is honest and loyal you will have difficulty feeling comfortable.

It is not unusual for you to have friends you have known since childhood. For you, there is a lot of value in the traditions and reliability of these life-long friendships. Introverted Organized Golds usually have a smaller group of close friends compared to Extraverts. Either way, your close friendships tend to last a lifetime.

When it comes to family relationships, you work hard to provide a loving and secure family environment. You feel a strong sense of responsibility towards family and you will often put family before everything and everyone else. You work hard at being a good friend, parent, and romantic partner, as well as being a caregiver to your parents. You may assume the traditional role of being the breadwinner, as well as taking on the primary responsibilities of caring for children and making a comfortable home.

You express your love and appreciation through actions. You worry about what people need from a practical point of view. You might show how much you care by making sure there is a hot and nutritious meal on the table each night, as opposed to showing affection. Or you may provide your partner with a safe, reliable car as a way of telling them that you love them, rather than using just words.

Loyalty is very important to you. You are loyal in all of your relationships and feel extremely disappointed if anyone lets you down. If you tell a friend you will meet them at a specific time and place, you will be there and you will also expect your friend to be there, and on time. You have high expectations of yourself as a friend and expect the same in return.

It takes time to earn your trust and respect. Once trust is given, it's given for life. However, if that trust is broken it is very difficult for you to trust or respect that person again.

Authentic Blue

 You value deep, meaningful relationships and tend to have long, lasting friendships. As a friend, you are there through thick and thin and are dependable no matter what. You feel fulfilled when you can support or encourage others - even as a parent - emotionally supporting your child through school transitions, breakups, and big life decisions. As a romantic partner, you support your spouse through big events in life, like the career change they have been dreaming of. You are a reliable friend and family member and will be there for others no matter what they need.

You are in tune to the needs of others and often put them ahead of your own. You are empathetic, caring, and supportive. If you sense that a person is hurting, you go out of your way to make them feel better. The Authentic Blues are the type of friends who will drop you off and pick you up from the airport even when it's not convenient for them. You are a friend in the truest meaning of the term and put your feelings into action.

When it comes to your romantic relationships, you need intimacy and authenticity, as well as thoughtfulness. A kind word or a small gesture means a lot to you. Giving and receiving back affection gives you confidence. You enjoy doing little things for other people and like it when others do the same for you. You are moved by acts of kindness and little things. You will often save the cards given to you by friends and family, regardless of the occasion.

Conflict can be very upsetting and hard for you. You tend to take criticism personally, and harsh words can cause you to feel hurt or disappointment. In your romantic relationships you can easily be hurt during an argument with your partner. While it is hard for both, Extraverted Authentic Blues are more likely to talk through conflict.

Because of your dislike of conflict, you are natural peacekeeper. That, along with your intuition, allows you to see and understand both sides of a conflict and help others come to a resolution.

Wouldn't it be amazing if all relationships were easy right from the start? However, as we already know, this isn't the case; if it was true, wouldn't life be boring?

Close personal relationships can be hard but at the same time, can also be also extremely rewarding. Understanding what you and the people you are close with need in a relationship will only strengthen your bond.

Conflict doesn't only exist in close personal relationships; it comes up in all areas of your life. In the next chapter you'll see some of the main causes of conflict for each of the four dimensions, and some ideas on how to overcome them.

6

In Conflict

When you are angry or feeling attacked, the last thing you do is stop and carefully think meaningfully about the 'best' way to respond. You just act! You have a tendency to go into autopilot and have it take over. You lead with your most preferred dimension, but not necessarily in a positive way and it may not be the best dimension for the situation. Start by reading your most preferred dimension first; it will give you a starting point for what causes you conflict and how you handle it.

As you know, the rest of who we are doesn't disappear when you're in a conflict situation - remember your plaid. As you read about the other dimensions you will be able to get a clearer picture of what you say and do in difficult situations. You will also be able to recognize the different dimensions others use when they have a conflict with you. Knowing why and how the four dimensions act while dealing with conflict, will give you a better understanding of why and how conflict gets started and how to manage it better.

Inquiring Green

What causes conflict for an Inquiring Green?

You pride yourself on your logical thinking and always work to put forward sensible arguments. People who respond irrationally frustrate and confuse you; especially if those responses are emotionally charged. If there are rules or restrictions that don't make sense, you are going to get your back up and look for a reason why they exist. If there isn't one, there is a good chance a conflict is going to happen.

What you know, and how much you know, is a point of pride for you. When your way of thinking is challenged, or people don't listen to your ideas, you may feel like your competence has been questioned. This goes over like a lead balloon.

You find people who repeat themselves or spend too much time going over (what you think are) unimportant details very frustrating. You need to see the big picture first before you can handle the details.

How Inquiring Greens cause conflict for others

The truth about Inquiring Greens is that you tend to communicate in an objective, non-emotional way. You may also fail to acknowledge other's feelings in emotionally charged situations. This can appear as detached, cold and uncaring and others may not feel heard or understood. Like Authentic Blues, you are a big-picture thinker, but friction can happen when they have outwardly emotional responses. You are not as comfortable experiencing them. It's a natural conflict between head and heart.

Because you think big picture, rather than being detail oriented, the Organized Golds or Resourceful Oranges, who like a more practical or concrete answer, can easily become annoyed and frustrated.

What Inquiring Greens look like when in conflict

You are often seen as ready for an argument. But it's not because you like to pick at people and get on their nerves. You enjoy bantering and debating and may even play devil's advocate just so that you can have a great discussion. Unfortunately, not everyone loves to be challenged and debated. You have a great poker face, and not showing your emotions makes some dimensions stressed and uncomfortable.

When you become emotional during a conflict you can feel vulnerable and out of control. You may have emotional outbursts or become very critical, or you might withdraw from a situation so you can compose yourself before you deal with the conflict. Unfortunately, others might assume that because you have withdrawn, you don't want to resolve the situation when that's not really the case. You just want some time to catch your breath so you can respond thoughtfully and logically – because that is the most comfortable way for you to manage conflict

Resourceful Orange

What causes conflict for a Resourceful Orange?

You are generally easy to get along with as long as you feel a sense of freedom. If you are given strict boundaries, you will likely push back. You do not like to be told what to do and micromanagement is a sure-fire way to get your back up.

Because you enjoy freedom, you are more likely to take risks and can become frustrated by people who insist on strict ways of doing things. In romantic partnerships, this can be a major source of conflict. If you are more daring and your partner is more reserved, critical or risk adverse this can sink your confidence.

You tend to use plain, straightforward language and make decisions quickly, and you can get frustrated with people who are long-winded and conceptual or who take a long time to make decisions.

How Resourceful Oranges cause conflict for others

One of the ways that you can create conflict is by bending the rules. As a teenager, you might have gotten into trouble with your parents or at school, because you may not have obeyed the rules, or you found ways to work around them. As an adult, you question established practices, and are comfortable with taking risks and embracing change.

Because you like to get things done quickly, you can clash with Inquiring Greens who are more focused on the process than the final result. In your push to get things done you sometimes miss out on including people in your decision making. This is a big point of conflict for Authentic Blues as they need to feel included. You may work best under pressure, but leaving things to the last-minute stresses out Organized Golds who are most confident creating a plan and sticking to it. If you get bored, there's a good chance you'll act out, or look for something else to do that is off task.

What Resourceful Oranges look like when in conflict

One of the strengths that you bring to a conflict situation is the ability to see all sides of the argument and then problem solve and negotiate a way to move forward.

You already know that life is short, so you don't like holding a grudge. You say what you have to say and then move on. However, others may not feel that the conflict is completely resolved, and this may cause additional conflict.

You can be very competitive, so you can sometimes continue an argument just to win; others can see this as combative.

Organized Gold

What causes conflict for an Organized Gold?

You love rules. Rules make your world go round. You get along just fine with fellow rule followers, but rule breakers? They may make you angry and frustrated. Disorganized people drive you crazy. At the end of the day, you like to tick all the boxes off your list and put everything in its place.

You are punctual (rule followers!) and are most likely to be 15 minutes early for every appointment. You also look at your watch with increasing levels of anger and frustration as you wait for late people to show up. You set high standards for yourself and expect others to have the same high standards. Remember the group work you had to do in school? You likely led the group and disapproved of the people who didn't work as hard as you did. You expected everyone in the group to have wanted an A and to have worked equally hard to make it happen.

You believe that clear leadership is important whether it is as a parent or as a boss. You can become frustrated when you have a poor leader who does not give clear directions or who procrastinates. You prefer clear instructions so you can be as successful as possible.

How Organized Golds cause conflict with others

Resourceful Oranges can find you too structured or detail oriented and feel like you sweat the small stuff. Inquiring Greens and Authentic Blues, who like the big picture, can get frustrated with someone who insists on checking every single box.

You are process oriented and have a hard time bending the rules. This can cause conflict with Authentic Blues who are more comfortable bending the rules if it puts people first.

You are quality motivated; you tend to keep checking in on others to make sure a job is done properly and on time. Resourceful Orange or Inquiring Green partners, children or employees can find this especially difficult since they want to get things done their way and not be micromanaged.

You tend to resist change at first (unless you are making the change yourself) and this can cause conflict with others. You may challenge why the change is necessary. This can be very frustrating, especially for other dimensions who readily embrace change. When things are changing, you can become uncomfortable. For you it is all about tradition and keeping things as they are unless there is a good reason to change!

What Organized Golds look like when in conflict

Overall, you want to bring conflicts out in the open so that you can problem solve with the other person and get things sorted out. You aren't conflict adverse, but you are most comfortable when you can work on resolving it right away. If you keep the conflict bottled up inside instead of dealing with it, this can take a toll on you.

Because trusting relationships are very important to you, you don't easily forgive if someone breaks that trust. The other person, regardless of their dimension, needs to work hard, and prove through their actions that they can be trusted again.

Authentic Blue

What causes conflict for an Authentic Blue?

You are caring and trusting and don't deal well with people who don't share this belief to the same extent. You are good at reading people and tend to sniff out someone who is dishonest quickly. Children of Authentic Blues sometimes think their parents can read their minds or have eyes in the backs of their heads.

You work hard at getting along with people, and find it stressful dealing with non-communicative or abrupt people. When you try to be nice, you expect others to be nice back. You thrive in a positive environment and tend to wilt when things get negative. You often struggle in a toxic environment and are less willing and emotionally able to be at your best. You can take criticism to heart and may not be able to deal with it in an objective way. If an Authentic Blue child has a critical parent, it will be harder for them to flourish. In the same way, a critical boss or romantic partner will not bring out the best in you. These kinds of relationships will drain your confidence.

How Authentic Blues cause conflict for others

You don't like conflict so sometimes bury your head in the sand and pretend that it doesn't exist. Avoiding is easier than facing conflict for you. Of course, the conflict doesn't disappear just because you stick your fingers in your ears and close your eyes. Inevitably, the conflict just grows and becomes much harder to deal with.

Your tendency to take things personally can cause conflict with others – especially Inquiring Greens who are more objective and less emotional. They can find your emotions hard to take. They just don't get what the big deal is; meanwhile you are frustrated as you feel that you aren't being understood. Even if your emotions are showing, your head can still be in the game.

Your overall approach involves making sure that everyone feels heard and understood, but it can be seen as overly time consuming and unnecessary to others. You clash with Resourceful Oranges when they overlook this with their drive to get things done. Conflict comes up with Organized Golds when they enforce rigid rules without thinking about how they affect everyone.

What Authentic Blues look like when in conflict

You tend to avoid conflict because you don't like to hurt peoples' feelings or see someone else stressed and upset. You have a high tolerance for other people's negative behaviour - even when hurt. You may not share your feelings because you do not want to anger the other person or cause unnecessary conflict. You'd rather just deal with it rather than let the other person know how bad you feel and risk hurting their feelings in the process. Extraverted Authentic Blues are more likely to openly share thoughts and feelings, and Introverted Authentic Blues are very uncomfortable being put on the spot in conflict situations.

When you work on resolving conflict, you do it in a very collaborative way. You are great at listening to the other person's side of the story, sharing your own thoughts and feelings, and working towards a win-win solution. Extraverts are more comfortable doing this face-to-face, while Introverts prefer using email and text messages to discuss difficult subjects.

Knowledge is power! Now that you have an understanding of how your dimension acts when in conflict you will be able to adjust your plaid when it doesn't serve you well. Knowing how the other dimensions act when in conflict helps you decide how to best approach a conflict with them.

Knowing what causes conflict between you and the other dimensions, and how to overcome it is another important step towards living life to its fullest. Being able to survive and thrive at work is the next. As you read the next chapter, think about how you can build on what you have learned up to this point.

7

At Work

Your success at work is based on who you are and how you make decisions. Do you get the job done right away or take your time? Do you like change or do you prefer the status quo? How do you get along with the people you didn't choose to be with? We all need to find a way to make it work. The first step is to understand how the different dimensions function at work so you can build on workplace strengths and reduce your challenges. Having an understanding of your co-workers' dimensions will help you appreciate their differences and understand their approach.

As you read this chapter, pay attention to your most preferred dimension and those of the people that you work with. As you read these pages it might be useful to think of someone in the workplace that you have difficulty communicating with, or work really well with. This might help you get into their brain a bit more, understand why they act the way they do, and maybe find a way to get along with your most challenging co-worker.

Inquiring Green

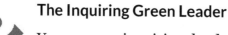

The Inquiring Green Leader

You are an inspiring leader who asks questions and seeks answers for different ways to do things. You feel confident making decisions when you ask questions, think logically through the pros and cons, and come up with the best solution.

You are an effective change agent and innovator who is open to new possibilities. Traditions or the past do not weigh heavily on you or your decisions. You like to invent new and better ways of doing things. You are at your best at the beginning stages of a project where you can look at the big picture, define the end goal, and figure out the best route to get there. Routine and repetition are hard for you, so you are more than happy to hand off a project once a plan is created.

You analyze situations in a logical way before you act, gathering all of the facts and data needed to ensure that you fully understand it; you don't just take things at face value. You question, research and challenge everything until you are confident that your facts are correct. As a big picture thinker, you relate information to underlying theories and philosophies from a number of sources. You use diagrams, flow charts, maps and other systematic tools to understand situations and explain them to others. You like to see things laid out and explained in a logical way.

You are a lifelong learner who likes to share what you know. You take pride in being an expert, and are happy to share your knowledge, principles and techniques with your employees. You will bring in outside experts, provide readings or new technology to help others learn. The more everyone knows, the better.

While you can come up with great ideas and approaches, you are not always great at communicating them. In fact, you can be confusing to others by being too abstract or overly technical. Because you don't like repetitiveness, you may only share your message once. In the workplace this can be especially frustrating for people who don't understand your message and don't get the opportunity to ask questions. Others can feel like they need to be mind-readers, increasing the risk or fear of getting it wrong.

You are good at many things, but you need reminders to be sensitive to others and recognize the importance of telling people they are doing a good job. Authentic Blues and Organized Golds especially find this difficult because they like to hear ongoing positive feedback. It lets others know that they are effective, appreciated and on the right page. You may not naturally tune into the feelings of others, because of this your employees may see you as distant and may avoid talking to you about important issues. But that doesn't mean you can't be supportive.

Being a perfectionist can make it hard for others to work for you. You can become irritated with employees who make mistakes or who ask you to repeat what you have already said. In the name of improvement, your natural tendency is to look for the flaws in everything and some employees can find this discouraging, because, well, it can be!

Tips for Working for an Inquiring Green Leader

Always present your ideas in a logical way. Do your best to show that you've put some thought into them, and have considered different things, and be confident with what you say. Make sure you get to the point from the get-go. Remember that most Inquiring Greens aren't into small talk, and be sure to communicate the big picture first before getting into details. Keeping future focussed is important too; you can honour the way things have been done in the past, but innovation is always on the top of Inquiring Greens' minds.

When you share your ideas with an Inquiring Green leader, be prepared for how they respond. Some people can see it as blunt, or critical. But that's not the case at all. Inquiring Greens are natural problem solvers who are driven to find answers and solutions. It helps if you can bring potential problems and solutions to the table when you're presenting your ideas. Inquiring Greens will want to debate them, but it's not personal. Being open to and exploring new ideas will help get to a better answer in the end. By understanding how Inquiring Greens work, you'll be able to keep your cool and avoid getting flustered.

The Inquiring Green Employee

You are always thinking about the future and you prefer to think about the big picture and approach ideas from an objective point of view. Complexity doesn't scare you off, and you thrive when analyzing and coming to your own conclusions. This can make you a great contributor to ideas that help manage change or uncertainty in the workplace. You can look at a situation from a strategic point of view and come up with new ways to overcome roadblocks and develop original solutions.

You are usually the one asking all the questions trying to find out what, why and how things work. Whether it is a mechanical problem, a process or a structure that needs to be designed, you are the right person for the job. You need the freedom to figure things out for yourself and then to act on what you have discovered. With the right freedom, you can be a major asset to any workplace.

For you, knowledge is power, and you have an ongoing need to learn new things; you are a lifelong learner. You are in your element when gathering information, analyzing it, strategizing and using it to create a new design, process, or structure. You like becoming involved in the early stage of a project where you can make the best use of your skills and creativity. However, you are not as interested in follow-through or implementing what you have created. That's why, as we mentioned earlier, you're happy to get the ball rolling and create a solid foundation for a project.

You base your decisions on facts, and you don't always naturally consider the emotional side of things. You are rational, logical, and skeptical; you're not willing to settle for the easy answer. Even if it seems logical to everyone else, you may continue to analyze information and look at a situation from all sides before making a final decision. For a room filled with people who just want to get something done, it can be difficult when you seem to spend too much time gathering and analyzing information.

You are more likely to have a dry sense of humour, which can rub some people the wrong way. You really need to know your audience, or you can come off as being sarcastic or cold. You're also not a huge fan of small talk. In a team setting, you can be seen as challenging by people who don't understand this is just the way you are. You don't mean to offend anyone. You enjoy a good discussion and debate in a cool, calm and collected manner. Because you have natural debating abilities and focus less on the emotions of others, you can come off as wanting to pick a fight, especially when you're stressed or out of esteem.

You have high expectations for yourself, and you sometimes find it hard to verbalize your own strengths. In other words, you might not even acknowledge how skilled and worthy you are. You do, however like it when you are recognized for your competence. If you are criticized, you prefer feedback that is direct, honest and precise with clear expectations for improvement.

Tips for Managing an Inquiring Green Employee

Remember that Inquiring Greens are always going to ask "why?" When you're giving instructions or assigning tasks, make sure you share your reasons. They aren't challenging your authority or trying to be difficult, they genuinely need to know to be motivated. Make sure your directions are presented in a logical way, and do your best to keep displays of emotion to a minimum. Keep the small talk to a minimum too.

Once an Inquiring Green knows what they need to do, leave them alone to get things done. You don't need to explain instructions again, or micromanage. If they have questions, they will come to you. That doesn't mean you can't check in from time-to-time and let them know you like what they're doing, but make sure to tell them why. Don't be put-off if they have a cool exterior; it just means that they're really focused on what they're doing.

Be prepared for Inquiring Greens to challenge the status quo, and come up with new ideas and solutions. Encourage them to be innovative and curious by giving them the opportunity to learn and take on new tasks. You'll find this leads to great results.

It's really important to recognize their competence, and at the same time help understand the impact they have on others. This keeps them focused and on track.

Resourceful Orange

The Resourceful Orange Leader

As a leader, you are an innovative problem solver who easily responds to changing situations. You are great at dealing with concrete problems and don't get preoccupied with the way things were done in the past. You need the freedom to experiment to solve problems and resolve issues. When there are problems, you don't sit there trying to analyze the situation. Your main goal is to get back on track.

You are at your best in crisis situations where quick, decisive action is needed. For example, rescuing a company from bankruptcy or working with a failing department to lead them back to success. You enjoy putting out fires and cleaning up messy situations. In these situations, you are able to make people believe in you, which encourages others to follow you. You prefer a fast paced, flexible work environment where there are tight deadlines and you have several things on the go at the same time.

As a gifted negotiator you can usually find the advantage and know what tactics to use to close a deal. To you negotiating is fun, almost like a game that you know how to play well. When it comes to organizational politics, you are a master at playing the political game.

As a coach, you like to motivate and excite others. You are more likely to demonstrate what to do rather than tell how to do it. You are a dedicated, hardworking leader and expect your followers to be the same. You thrive as a motivator and cheerleader.

You are energized by change. As a Resourceful Orange, you look for ways to make things go smoother or quicker. You like to add an element of fun to everything you do. You aren't the type of person who gets hung up on things you know you can't do anything about. You're not big on sweating the small stuff; you focus on the things you can control. You are willing to change course as necessary, and invite others to come along for the ride, no matter which way it goes. Of all the dimensions you are the most willing to take risks when making change and will encourage others to do so as well.

One thing that sets you apart in the boardroom is that you are often looked to as being a change agent – you can be convincing and persuasive and are quick on your feet in a verbal sparring match. At the same time, you can often work out a deal that all team members can agree on. That doesn't mean you're all serious and all business. In fact, quite the opposite is true! You tend to have a great sense of humour. Your humour, sense of camaraderie and optimism allows you to be the type of leader that moves the team forward, especially during difficult and stressful times.

As leaders, you can pay a heavy price for the fact that you don't need a well-thought-out plan to try to move things forward. Sometimes, you act too quickly without looking at or considering the big picture and that can come back to bite you. Some of your short-term solutions can lead to long-term complications. While you're pretty good at getting a plan up and running, you aren't necessarily as great at the follow through. This could mean some things simply fall through the cracks.

You can come across as being blunt and be seen as pushy when seeking a decision; but really you just want to get things done. You can also become confrontational and impulsive when dealing with opposition when you're stressed. You find it difficult when others don't keep up with your fast pace, focus on every detail or get frustrated by your short-term approach.

While you can be a great trouble-shooter, you are less great at maintaining the status quo in an organization. Because you avoid routine and fight against rigid boundaries, you can come off as unpredictable, unprepared and even irresponsible. The last thing you want to do is follow rules, procedures and routines that are dictated to you, when you are always looking for positive change.

Tips for Working for a Resourceful Orange Leader

Resourceful Oranges are motivated to get things done, and move on to the next. You need to present your ideas in clear, practical language, and get to the point quickly. Show how your ideas have concrete, real-life benefits, and avoid conceptual thinking. It doesn't hurt to use some humour too if it's appropriate in the situation. Try to be open to change; Resourceful Oranges like finding new ways of doing things, and aren't as tied to the past.

Show that you are adaptable and use your initiative. Don't wait to react to things, be proactive and look for solutions before problems happen. You aren't going to be closely supervised by Resourceful Oranges. Once you've been assigned a task or given instructions, don't wait around for more if they're not clear. You're going to have to ask, but that's okay. They would rather give information on demand then spend time covering every possible detail at the start.

You will win over a Resourceful Orange by showing off your skills in high-pressure or crisis situations. Keep in mind that they can come across as abrasive in these situations, but for them it's about getting their point across efficiently. Resourceful Oranges recognise the value of dedicated work, but there's nothing that says you can't have fun while doing it. They are naturally competitive, and it comes across in their leadership style; be prepared to work hard and play hard.

The Resourceful Orange Employee

You work hard and take pride in getting things right the first time. You do great in fast-paced workplaces that give you the freedom to do the job the way you think makes the most sense. You get frustrated and stressed if you are micromanaged or told what to do. You do well when given a deadline and are left alone to get the job done.

Time and freedom are very important to you. You can get bored easily and like to be kept busy. If you find yourself with time on your hands you will look for ways to fill it by taking on additional tasks or helping others. If you can't find something to fill your time you are at risk of finding unproductive ways to keep you occupied.

You like it when things change at work. In fact, you thrive on new challenges and the opportunity to develop more skills. You are often the one who will jump at an opportunity to take on a new assignment. You will have no problem making suggestions and pointing out ways to make things look and work better.

You like to live life to its fullest with a balance between work and fun. You look for ways to make your workplace more fun. Whether it is turning the task at hand into a competition of some kind, being part of the social committee, or decorating the office during a holiday season you just want to make life as enjoyable as possible for everyone. Being at work is not a reason to be serious and focused all the time for you. You see the ability to have fun at work as a way to inspire and energize the people around you.

Crisis situations are totally in your wheelhouse. How you show it depends on how Introverted or Extraverted you are. Your ability to observe, assess, and analyze a situation in the moment enables you to make quick decisions and act on them. In a fast-paced or crisis environment, like an emergency room or a newsroom, where there are tight deadlines, you can be extremely useful. You shine if you are in a position where you can lead the team through the situation.

You tend to make decisions quickly and don't like to waste time with a lengthy decision-making process. An office that has a million meetings would be a nightmare for you; you just want to get to work. You don't see the need for drawn-out discussions, decisions by committee or multiple layers of approvals. As a natural risk taker, you are known to voice your impatience which can cause others to get frustrated.

You excel when you can use your creative and persuasive skills. Your ability to determine what someone wants allows you to work creatively to persuade them that an idea or product will meet their needs. These skills also work well for you in negotiations. You like to negotiate from a win/win perspective ensuring that the needs of everyone are met.

Tips for Managing a Resourceful Orange Employee

Resourceful Oranges need the freedom and space to do what they do. You will get their best work if you avoid micromanaging them. Only give them information that is useful and necessary to get the job done; tell them what you want to get accomplished, not how to do it. Be prepared to answer their questions using plain, clear language, and get to the point quickly when they ask them. It's okay to check in every now and then to give words of encouragement, and have some fun with it. Resourceful Oranges appreciate it when you can throw in some humor.

When assigning tasks, keep in mind the kinds of work where Resourceful Oranges shine. They are great in crisis situations, and readily embrace change. They need variety to be fulfilled; give them different tasks and assignments as much as possible. Both Introverts and Extraverts like and need action; Extraverts prefer their action to be people oriented. Keep your Resourceful Oranges happy by creating a relaxed and friendly environment. Let them have some fun while they get their work done. Set clear deadlines, and challenge them to friendly competitions.

Organized Gold

The Organized Gold Leader

Your biggest strength as a leader is your ability to make sure that an organization runs smoothly and efficiently. You work within the existing organizational structure to make plans to achieve clear goals and objectives for your team. To make sure everyone is on the same page about what is expected, you develop clear procedures, rules and guidelines. You provide a stable, secure workplace where everyone knows what to expect. You are loyal to both your employees and the organization.

As leaders, you have high standards for yourself and others. You believe in continuous improvement, and are an effective coach, by showing how things should be done. You are good at monitoring and managing the work of others. When you find a mistake, you are often quick to let your employees know. You can come across as overly critical because it may seem to others that nothing is ever good enough for you. In fact, you believe something can always be done better. Because criticism comes easier to you than praise, you need to remember to give positive feedback when people do a good job. As a realist you know that at any time, anything can go wrong, so you are naturally cautious and security minded. You always try to predict what could go wrong and put contingency plans in place to maintain a stable workplace. The motto 'Always be Prepared' was likely coined by an Organized Gold.

You are decisive, practical and do not suffer from analysis paralysis. However, because you are cautious you need to make sure you have enough information to make a sound decision. At the same time, you don't want to get bogged down with information that isn't relevant or important. When making decisions you take into account available information, possible alternatives, past experiences and work constraints.

You focus on the here and now, and aren't as concerned with an overall vision. You are more comfortable focusing on the past and the present than on the future. Unlike Inquiring Greens or Authentic Blues, you don't focus as much on new possibilities and realities in the future. As a leader you need to use your plaid to consider the big picture and future direction of the organization rather than the details of the past or present.

You can seem rigid and resistant to change. You don't just jump on the bandwagon; you need to be convinced that a change is good and will lead to improvement. You are cautious because you want to hold on to what has worked in the past and not make a change for changes sake. New doesn't always mean better. If you don't see value in a change, you are less likely to adopt it. Once you see the value you will want to know the what, when and how the change will be implemented and then you will be excellent at making the change happen.

On a leadership team you provide the voice of practicality and common sense. You also make sure that all important details are considered. In constantly changing times, you provide a necessary stability – challenging change for the sake of change and making sure that your team does not forget the important traditions of an organization. If the organization does not have traditions, like holiday parties, for example, you like to create them.

Tips for Working for an Organized Gold Leader

Organized Golds are motivated by rules, standards, and procedures in the workplace. It is important that you respect traditions and the way things have been done in the past. You can be creative, just make sure you present your ideas in a detailed, step-by-step way. Be open to criticism, but know that it isn't personal. Organized Golds want to share their wealth of experience.

To stay on an Organized Gold leader's good side, keep your workspace tidy and organized. Be on-time for the start of the work day, and ready to get down to work. Try your best to do work in a systemic way, and complete your tasks on time, seeing things through to completion.

Show your loyalty to them, and they will reciprocate. Organized Golds are team players, and expect the same out of everyone. Do what you say you are going to do, and keep your word.

The Organized Gold Employee

If a well-organized effective administrator is needed, you are the person to hire. You are great at organizing things and are very good at getting the job done when you understand the process, have clear checkpoints and a deadline. You often like to work in administrative jobs, especially in the fields of medicine, public education and social services.

Doing a job effectively and being rewarded for your efforts are meaningful and empowering to you. You want to feel like you are an important part of the workplace, helping to ensure it runs smoothly and efficiently. You aim to be a successful and productive member of any team. As a team member, you are conscientious, helpful and focused on getting the job done.

You have a strong sense of community and tradition and bring it to any role. You can be counted on to do things like putting up holiday decorations in the office and volunteering to help make co-workers feel part of the team. You are an important team member because of your loyalty, dependability, and commitment to getting the job done.

You are the most comfortable working in organizations that have a set structure and hierarchy - one with clear boundaries, set expectations and timelines. You respond well to and respect authority. If you know that the person asking you to do something is in a position of authority, you will comply. When being assigned a task, you prefer to know what the task is, how to do it, when it is due, and what the budget is that you have to work with. If you know all of the details, you will do your best to complete the task successfully and on time.

You can be resistant to workplace change if you don't see how it will benefit the organization. That said, once you understand why the change is needed, you will use your organizational skills to ensure that it is done properly. You are the one who creates the new policies and procedures to make it go smoothly.

You have the tendency to worry about things not going to plan. Not having a backup, just in case, gives you stress. As does change without a good reason. When you're stressed or out of esteem you have can be self-critical, and overly critical of others.

You are often motivated by praise, tangible rewards and recognition. You like to be recognized verbally for a job well done. You also appreciate things like: a plaque, a gift card, being taken out to dinner with your team, or a company trip.

Overall, you make a great addition to any workplace and without you many would fall apart. You keep the work world running smoothly.

Tips for Managing an Organized Gold Employee

Organized Golds need clear expectations, a sense of structure, and organization to be fulfilled at work. It is important that you communicate clearly, logically, and sequentially on the what, when, and how of tasks. Providing an organized workspace where everything has its place, with clear policies and procedures will allow them to succeed.

Organized Golds need a secure, stable work environment, but that doesn't mean they can't embrace change. When it comes time to implement change, it is important to present it as an opportunity. Help them understand why change has to occur for practical reasons. Build trust with Organized Golds by following through with your promises and commitments.

When handing out tasks, remember that Organized Golds like routine, and practical work they can see through to the end. Give them opportunities for purposeful and meaningful service. Recognize their efforts with more than words; a lunch out, extra time off, or awards/certificates.

Authentic Blue

The Authentic Blue Leader

You have a great ability to motivate and inspire others to be their best. You use your innate ability to identify each individual's true potential both for current and future positions. As a leader you are at your best when coaching or mentoring people. You have patience and a willingness to help people develop their strengths so they can thrive at work. You motivate and encourage others by giving positive recognition for both working towards and achieving goals. You work with your employees to help them find new career opportunities and continue to mentor them long after they have moved on to other positions.

Your leadership style is participative. You develop a team-based workplace where everyone works together to reach consensus on key issues. You like to create a comfortable climate where people feel safe to share their thoughts, ideas, and feelings. Once a consensus has been reached, you are happy to let each employee decide how to best reach their individual goals. You don't tend to micromanage because you'd rather not get into the finer details.

You have a great ability to see the big picture and use your gift with words to inspire others by creating a vision that they want to follow. Because you can bring together different pieces of information and have an overall sense of what is happening, you often see the best path for the organization to follow. By using metaphors, stories and symbols you can paint a picture of what you want to achieve.

You can make a real contribution during times of change. When carrying out workplace change you will spend time communicating change in such a way that you get buy-in and commitment. You are also sensitive to the needs of your employees and will bring their views to the table as the organization plans and carries out change. You will spend the time needed to handle individual concerns - helping employees adapt to and accept the change.

Because you tend to shy away from conflict more than the other dimensions, you find it hard to deal with employees who are not performing well. You have a tendency to avoid addressing it, hoping that the person will improve on their own. If that does not work (and it often doesn't), you will spend a lot of time and energy coaching the employee to improve. You tend to have emotional reactions to situations, and this can be seen as a weakness by both your employees and management. You can be seen as too emotional by Inquiring Greens, and this may also be seen as a weakness by Resourceful Oranges and Organized Golds. But this is just how you express yourself.

As a leader, you have to be careful not to burn out because you are so in tune with your employees. You are willing to take the time to listen to any of your employees' concerns, since you feel comfortable in the counselling role. However, this will give you less time to focus on workplace priorities or your own personal life.

Tips for Working for an Authentic Blue Leader

Authentic Blue leaders like it when their teams are able to work cohesively. To them, a happy team is a productive team. They appreciate it when team members are able to work out interpersonal conflicts on their own. When working with them, don't forget to take the time for the niceties; ask how they are and take the time to actively listen.

When you're approaching an Authentic Blue leader with ideas make sure you aren't too direct. Take your time to explain the big picture before getting down to the fine details. Be imaginative; use stories, metaphors, and analogies. Adding in personal examples helps to get your point across. Stay focused on the future, and don't dwell on the past.

Whatever kind of work you're doing, be authentic; demonstrate that you believe in the work you are doing, and how it will have a positive impact on other people. Authentic Blue leaders like to discuss what you are working on, but may be hesitant to provide feedback because they don't want to come across as critical. You may need to directly ask for their input.

The Authentic Blue Employee

As an employee you prefer to work in an environment that is cohesive and creative. You like being able to interact with co-workers not only from a workplace perspective but also from a personal one. You like to know your co-workers and understand them as people, their backgrounds, families, likes and dislikes, interests and abilities. You form relationships with your co-workers, managers, customers and anyone who you have ongoing contact with. People tend to find you easy to talk to, a good listener and safe to confide in. It can be difficult if you find yourself working where this is not allowed, you may become lonely and stressed.

You are good at motivating and inspiring others to be their best. You are generous with giving positive and constructive feedback in a way that is helpful and supportive. You thrive on receiving positive recognition and without it, can often assume the worst, and doubt your abilities.

You are genuine with others, but you don't just 'tell it like it is' because you also care about the emotional well-being of others. As a result, you will do anything to avoid inflicting emotional pain. To you, honesty means dealing with others fairly and not manipulating them in any way. You are wary of people who you don't think are being honest and you aren't a fan of giving or receiving brutal honesty. You don't mind receiving feedback. But the delivery of the message needs to be constructive and fair.

You are very supportive of workplace change if you believe it is in the best interests of the employees and aligns with your values. Because of your sensitivity to the needs of others, you are helpful in identifying how people are responding to change. You can also suggest what needs to be put in place to help them to feel comfortable with the new direction. If workplace support is not given, it causes a hit to your confidence and self-esteem.

You find situations where you need to pay particular attention to detail difficult. Because you think big picture, you prefer to leave the details to others. If you really need to you can focus on details - by using the other colours in your plaid.

You generally think about the future rather than the present or past, you find it difficult when you constantly need to focus on what is happening in the here and now or on practical realities.

Because of your creativity and connection with others, you are a productive and inspiring team member. You can help motivate teams and get everyone working together. You provide emotional support to teammates, especially when things aren't going well. You are good at coming up with creative and inventive solutions to whatever problems your team is facing. You are a flexible team member who is willing to help wherever needed.

You are good at speaking and writing. You like having the opportunity to express yourself in creative and artistic ways and you might be attracted to careers in the arts, entertainment, media or marketing.

You enjoy working with people, and are drawn to service-oriented, teaching, healing or helping professions. In these roles you use your skills of seeing the big picture and being empathetic, caring and intuitive to help people grow and develop.

Tips for Managing an Authentic Blue Employee

Authentic Blues do their best work when they are part of a collaborative process. When you give instructions or delegate tasks don't go straight to the details; explain the overall scope first and then drill down to the specifics when needed. You'll get great buy-in from Authentic Blues if you explain how the final result will have a positive impact on others. Use personal examples, metaphors and analogies to illustrate your points. Authentic Blues are great ideas people who are naturally creative and can see the big picture. Extroverts are quicker to share their ideas in meetings and brainstorming sessions, so make sure you give Introverts time and space to present theirs and their creativity will come through,

It is important to respect the emotional needs of Authentic Blues. They are known for wearing their hearts on their sleeves. Be genuine, listen to them when they are upset and let them share their emotions if needed. It's not about solving their issues; it's about giving them space to get things off their chest. Always recognize Authentic Blues for their contributions with a few words of appreciation and encouragement along the way.

How you act at work is an extension of who you are. Your values, natural talents, and needs are all reflected in the work you do. Some people work to live, and others live to work. Regardless of your most preferred dimension, being in a workplace that supports these allow you to live life to its fullest.

A workplace made up of all the dimensions, both Introverted and Extraverted uses everyone's strengths and talents to do great things. Disagreements and friction are normal, but it's up to leaders and co-workers to use your understanding of Personality Dimensions to keep things running smoothly.

How do you know what someone else's preferred communication style is if you don't really know them? The next chapter will give you some clues on how to figure this out.

8

Your Personality Radar

Being able to understand how people work is one of the most important skills to live life to its fullest. You need to know core needs, values, strengths and weaknesses, and how to communicate effectively. Everyone is unique, and you can get valuable insight into them by working out their dimensions, and their tendency towards Introversion or Extraversion using your Personality Radar. Tuning into your Personality Radar means picking up on the visual, verbal, and non-verbal cues you see in other people. It's not an exact science, since you can only pick up on what you're presented with, but as you spend more time with other people, the better the picture your Personality Radar will give you. When you have it figured out, you will be able to better communicate, influence, and build stronger relationships with others. As you read through the chapter start thinking about the cues you give off, and the ones you pick up from the people in your life.

Inquiring Green

 Inquiring Greens make up the smallest portion of the population. Only about 20% of Canadians have Inquiring Green as their most preferred dimension. This can make them a little easier to detect. When talking with an Inquiring Green, you will notice that they aren't as focused on little details, but rather on the big picture. They're more interested in how things unfold in the future, and not the past, or even the here-and-now. Inquiring Greens make decisions based on facts, and tend to operate in a pretty logical way.

Introverted Inquiring Greens are more focused on their inner world, so appearance tends not to be as much of a priority. They may not even be aware of the way they look. Albert Einstein was a genius, but he certainly didn't look that way. Extraverts, on the other hand tend to focus more energy on the way that they look because they believe it shows their success. For example, some wear designer clothes, belong to exclusive social groups, and drive nice cars; tangible things that show personal success.

For the most part, Inquiring Greens present a calm, collected demeanor. Outwardly they often show that they are rational and in control of themselves. They don't tend to use excessive arm gestures or body movements, and when they do it is very intentional. Because showing excessive emotion makes Inquiring Greens feel vulnerable, they typically do not show a lot of emotion on their faces, or in their tone of voice. When stressed or out of esteem, the opposite can be true.

Inquiring Greens usually have large vocabularies and tend to use precise language, especially when it comes to work, or things they are passionate about. Because their thought processes can be pretty complex, they can present a lot of ideas at the same time with the expectation that others keep up. This isn't done intentionally to confuse or frustrate others, it's just what comes naturally. They enjoy playing with words. Inquiring Greens use a lot of puns, complex terms and double meanings. When communicating, they tend to present their points logically.

Inquiring Greens can be skilled communicators; Introverts are more talented with the written word, while Extraverts are more talented with speech. Either way, how they construct their messages are the same. Inquiring greens like to use models, and diagrams to explain complex ideas. They're also good at using analogies and metaphors to help explain things.

Inquiring Greens generally appear to be competent people who are confident in their own abilities. They like to be with people who are well respected and tend to stay away from people that they don't hold in high regard. Of all the dimensions, they are the best at debating and critiquing the ideas of others; they are naturally able to see things others have missed and consider alternatives. They really enjoy taking on the role of devil's advocate in a playful way, but unfortunately this can come across as arrogant or dismissive to others.

Inquiring Greens often put a lot of priority on their careers and spend a lot of time working towards improving their skills so they can advance. Their drive for continual learning and improvement can make them fall into a pattern of neglecting other areas of life. Learning is a great passion; Inquiring Greens like to take courses, read articles on the internet, listen to podcasts or read books to increase their knowledge. Anything that helps to build their knowledge and skillset.

Inquiring Greens like to focus on hobbies where they can challenge themselves and apply their knowledge, skill, and strategic thinking. Strategy-based games like chess, Monopoly, and Trivial Pursuit are favourites. They are also attracted to sports like golf, badminton, or skiing because they can use their minds and physical abilities to master them.

Resourceful Orange

 Resourceful Oranges have a down-to-earth, practical approach to life. About 25% of Canadians have Resourceful Orange as their most preferred dimension. They tend to focus on life's details; what is going on in the present. Resourceful Oranges are happy with a last-minute change of plans and really welcome change. To a Resourceful Orange, life is an experience, and it is meant to be lived in the here and now. They thrive on action and variety, and aim to experience life, not just live it.

Resourceful Oranges like to dress comfortably, allowing them room to move, but this doesn't necessarily mean they dress casually; for example, preferring to carry a knapsack instead of a brief case since it's more comfortable to carry. They like to look good but in an easygoing way. Both Introverts and Extraverted Resourceful Oranges like to look good, and set themselves apart. They like to accessorize, with jewelry, glasses, or makeup as long as it doesn't get in the way of feeling comfortable or being able to freely move.

Resourceful Oranges are very aware of their bodies and tend to be conscious of how they move. For the most part, they give the impression that they are very comfortable in their own skin. Resourceful Oranges need to move, even in confined spaces. They can get fidgety when there isn't a lot going on, and usually find something to play with, like a pen or small change, to keep their hands busy and engaged.

A more casual, uncomplicated communication style is preferred by Resourceful Oranges. While they may have a lot to say, their sentence structure tends to be free flowing. They are usually up on the latest slang for their age group and are comfortable using it.

Resourceful Oranges don't like to hang around or waste time in anything they do, so they speak in a succinct way and aren't big fans of chit chat and small talk. They would rather talk about real things and events, rather than ideas and concepts. When explaining something, they like to make use of real-life experiences, either their own or those of others. Resourceful Oranges like to use sports and other real-world events metaphors to make things easier to understand.

Relaxed is really the best way to describe how Resourceful Oranges present themselves. Just be careful to not confuse relaxed with laziness. Resourceful Oranges may be relaxed, but they are action-oriented, and want to get things done. They have an easy going, uncomplicated, and happy approach to life. They very much live in the present and are pretty aware of what is going on around them. Resourceful Oranges are always ready to respond no matter what the situation. If you find yourself in a crisis, Resourceful Oranges are good to have around because they are usually pretty cool headed, and don't get flustered easily.

Resourceful Oranges are action-oriented. They like activities that involve movement, whether it is of the whole body or just working with their hands. For the most part, they love to either play or at least be involved in sports of some kind, and tend to stay at work beyond their retirement years.

Resourceful Oranges are naturally competitive; they are drawn to sports. There's a misconception that they are adrenaline junkies, but it's really about the movement and the challenge involved. Everything from soccer to skydiving attracts Resourceful Oranges. Different levels of intensity appeal to different abilities and life stages. In addition to sports, they also like a variety of games - the more active the better. For example, a Resourceful Orange is more likely to enjoy a game of Twister than they are a game of Scrabble.

Often very good at using tools, Resourceful Oranges are drawn to hobbies like home renovations, metal working, or gardening; anything that involves working with their hands.

Organized Gold

 Organized Golds focus on facts, data and specifics. A little over 20% of Canadians have Organized Gold as their most preferred dimension. They go about things in a practical way and don't tend to stray too far from what makes good sense. They live in the moment and draw on the past to make decisions. Organized Golds are prepared and efficient; they excel at planning and organizing, and they are very comfortable working with rules, standards and procedures. They are punctual and hold others to the same standards they create for themselves.

Organized Golds present themselves to the world in a more traditional way that is appropriate to the situation and environment they are in. They don't devote a lot of time or energy to the latest trends and styles; they would prefer to present themselves as neat and well-dressed people who do not stand out in a crowd. For the most part, they have tidy, well styled hair, and neat, well-coordinated clothes and shoes. Their overall presentation suggests someone who is well put together. Practicality is very important and they would generally prefer to wear something that is comfortable rather than stylish. Finding something that is both is an achievement for Organized Golds.

The body language of Organized Golds reflects their practical, matter of fact approach to life. They don't tend to be expressive or flamboyant with their physical gestures, or use excessive body movements. Organized Golds are traditionalists; when meeting them for the first time, you can expect to see good eye-contact and a firm handshake in formal and informal settings. They strongly believe in politeness. They greet people, say goodbye, hold doors and happily take their place in line. Generally, Organized Golds' tone of voice is well controlled and clear so that others can understand the message they are trying to get across.

When communicating in person or in writing, Organized Golds use words that tend to reflect the practical, no-nonsense type of people they are. They carefully use clear, easily understood words to get their message across. Organized Golds usually relate information to their own past experience. For example, they might say "From my experience..." or "In the past... ". Information is laid out in a logical, step-by-step way, focusing on facts and details.

Extraverted Organized Golds can be quite talkative, but both they and Introverted Organized Golds conversations focus on facts, details and information. Their writing style is clear, logical and to the point, outlining the necessary information in detail.

Organized Golds come across as responsible, serious people who do what they say they are going to do. That's not to say they don't like to have a good time; they just need to get work out of the way before they can comfortably play. They believe in hierarchy, rules, standards and procedures and work effectively within this kind of structure. Organized Golds are cooperative, and always willing to help to get the job done. They prioritize common sense, and usually show it through their actions.

Organized Golds have a strong sense of duty, like to belong and be included in work and social activities. They tend to prefer routine, and don't always like to change from the way things were done in the past. They usually have specific ideas about how things should be done.

Organized Golds need to belong to groups and are driven by giving time and energy to their community. They are talented organizers and can be found doing volunteer work for community groups, local hospital, or service organizations. As parents, they are often on the parent-teacher association; they volunteer for guides/scouts or coach their children's sports teams. At work Organized Golds meet their social needs by volunteering to work on social groups and extracurricular activities.

Organized Golds have many different hobbies that usually involve being part of an organization. Both Introverted and Extraverted Organized Golds have the need to belong and maintain meaningful connections. They enjoy activities where they can be physical such as team sports, gardening or hiking. Others enjoy using their hands to do arts and crafts or other activities that produce a useable product.

Authentic Blue

Authentic Blues focus their attention on people and relationships. They make up the largest chunk of the population, with about 35% of Canadians identifying Authentic Blue as their most preferred dimension. They value their uniqueness and originality. Authentic Blues write and speak well, are good listeners and engage people in productive dialogue. They focus on the big picture, and the future; always looking for ways to make things better for the people around them. It's important to Authentic Blues that the people in their lives get along, be it at work or at home. They can be deeply spiritual and their spiritual path may be traditional or untraditional.

Authentic Blues value being unique and original, they don't like to dress like everyone else. They often wear clothes, jewelry, shoes, or accessories that make a statement about who they are. Authentic Blues are free-thinkers who have fun with their appearance. They often like to wear funky clothes and accessories that express who they are – picking up bits and pieces at a vintage store, a boutique, or from a close acquaintance. Regardless of what pieces Authentic Blues choose to wear, they are creatively and stylistically well put together.

For the most part, Authentic Blues are very expressive, using grand arm gestures, body movement and facial expressions to get their ideas across. They often express themselves passionately when talking about something they believe in. Introverted Authentic Blues may not demonstrate this as much, especially if they haven't had time to recharge.

At times, Authentic Blues can get so caught up in their own world that they can seem slightly clumsy. As a result, they may bump into a table or trip over something on the floor. They have the tendency to daydream, and get caught up in their own thoughts and possibilities, not being fully aware of the world around them. That being said Authentic Blues generally convey warmth by smiling or leaning in towards the person they are speaking to in order to show that they are listening.

Authentic Blues are known to speak well, especially when they are talking about big picture ideas, personal concerns, or relationships. They often choose expressive words to convey emotion and to make an impact on others. Authentic Blues are gifted at using metaphors, analogies and personal experiences as a way of explaining their point of view. Their writing tends to be flowing and colourful, and at times, a little on the wordy side. Authentic Blues prefer to talk in generalities rather than specifics. In fact, they can find it difficult to give precise information such as directions or a detailed description of an event that has occurred.

Authentic Blues are best described as warm and nurturing people. They excel at listening and giving empathy to others – especially when talking about personal issues. At times, they don't hesitate to share personal information about themselves or ask others questions about their personal lives. It's not to be nosy, but is done out of genuine interest and concern for other people. Both Introverted and Extraverted Authentic Blues can easily meet people and have in-depth conversations about their lives without knowing the other person well, or at all. Extraverts just have the energy on hand to do it. Introverts need to get to know the other person before they will share details about their life. Either way, Authentic Blues can get caught up in conversations that focus on personal issues, self-development, their values or helping others.

They are the most comfortable when talking about big picture plans and ideas. Because they see connections between ideas that others do not see as easily, they may appear to jump from one idea to another. Since Authentic Blues can be lost in their world of thoughts, they can appear as though they are detached from reality and even a little dreamy.

Authentic Blues love to engage in meaningful conversations with others where they can be truly authentic. Personal growth is a passion; they enjoy reading self-help books, attending courses or talking to others who can help them grow as individuals. Authentic Blues need to believe in what they do, be it at work or in their spare time. They are often devoted to helping others or causes that will help humanity. They are very willing to help friends, associates, and clients by coaching and supporting them, and get great satisfaction from helping others grow and reach their full potential.

Naturally creative with thoughts, ideas and words, Authentic Blues enjoy thinking outside of the box or doing creative activities like writing, performing, or acting. They may enjoy team sports where there is a sense of comradery and individual and group achievements can be celebrated.

Your Personality Radar isn't an exact science; you can only look at and understand what is being presented to you. Remember, you don't always use your most preferred dimension; sometimes you need to use your plaid in different situations, so that can throw off your Personality Radar. More often than not, you use your most preferred dimension when you are in a comfortable environment. This may or may not be at work, at home with family, or some social situations, so it gets a little tricky. The more others get to know you and the more you get to know others, you will see preferred dimensions start to stand out. Once you have a better idea of how others think and act, you will be able to communicate and get along better, strengthening your relationships to new levels.

As you start to fine tune your Personality Radar, you'll notice that the dimensions actually have a lot of similarities in certain areas, but can be very different in others. In the next, and final chapter you'll see how to tie it all together, and make sense of what all of this means.

9

Tying it all Together

As you've been making your way through this book, you've been discovering a lot about yourself, and the others around you. You've likely noticed that the dimensions actually have a lot in common in many ways, but there's also some pretty big differences. So how does this all work in the real world? As you read this chapter think about the important people in your life; you will begin to understand what you have in common and what some of the challenges might be.

Similarities

Authentic Blues and Resourceful Oranges share an outlook on people; both are socially-oriented and tend to be good problem-solvers and negotiators. They are able to see all sides of an issue and can be very fair when dealing with problems. Authentic Blues bring their collaborative skills to the table and will generally work towards a mutual solution. Resourceful Oranges are masters at negotiating. They understand the give and take of a negotiation and have a 6th sense about what to say so that a deal is reached. Both dimensions are natural optimists; with their first inclination being to look for the positives in different situations.

Both Authentic Blues and Resourceful Oranges like to experience a lot of different things in life, and don't feel the need to specialize in a certain area. You are kind of "Jack-of-all-trades, master of none" types. Once you've tried something out to the point of getting good at it, you tend move on to something else. It's not so much the activity itself that you're after, it's the experience of trying something new that keeps life interesting.

Authentic Blues and Resourceful Oranges both like and need recognition. However, the way that they like to be recognized is different. Authentic Blues prefer a "thank you" to be either verbally or in writing. Resourceful Oranges, on the other hand, like tangible rewards like a gift or time off.

Inquiring Greens and Organized Golds both are natural critics, but that's because you have high expectations. However, you tend to critique different things. Organized Golds are more likely to critique the way another person is performing a task or plan. An Inquiring Green on the other hand is more likely to see the gaps in a person's logic. You bring balance because you help point out the possible pitfalls in a situation. It is very important for Inquiring Greens and Organized Golds to do a good job and produce a quality product. Inquiring Greens need to feel knowledgeable and competent and Organized Golds need to know that they have followed the rules and done the best job they can.

Inquiring Greens and Organized Golds are both quality conscious and work hard to produce excellent results. You like to specialize and get really good in certain areas. You both feel like you can always improve, no matter how good you are at something.

Inquiring Greens and Resourceful Oranges value their independence. While you can work on teams, you do your best when given the freedom and space to create. You only need to be told what needs to be done once; if you have follow-up questions, or need more information, you will ask for it.

Inquiring Greens and Resourceful Oranges both like to find new ways to do things. Inquiring Greens use their ingenuity and set the bar higher by improving a product or the way things are done. Resourceful Oranges like do things differently to avoid boredom and to find efficiencies.

Authentic Blues and Organized Golds are very concerned about creating, developing, and maintaining different kinds of relationships; Authentic Blues, because it is your core need to connect with others and Organized Golds, because you like to nurture a sense of belonging. Both of you relate well to people, are helpful and co-operative and do your best to avoid conflict.

Authentic Blues and Organized Golds both have a strong sense of social responsibility. Organized Golds are more drawn to established groups and institutions; you take pride in contributing your time to coach sports teams, volunteer at the library or an arts organization. Authentic Blues are more likely to direct efforts to causes like fundraising for charities, volunteering for homeless organizations, and helping others in need in the community.

Inquiring Greens and Authentic Blues are both very creative, although how they display this creative is unique. Inquiring Greens are innovative and visionary, and Authentic Blues are often more aesthetic and artistic. Both of you are big picture-oriented and don't focus as much on little details. Both of you are process-oriented; Inquiring Greens more so with systems and how things are working, and Authentic Blues with how the people will be affected by what's happening.

Organized Golds and Resourceful Oranges are more task-oriented. Both of you just want to get the job done and prefer concrete and practical to abstract and theoretical. Compared to the "big-picture" way that Inquiring Greens and Authentic Blues think, both the Organized Golds and Resourceful Oranges are more focused on the here and now.

Both Organized Golds and Resourceful Oranges are able to take on a project and run with it. Organized Golds will create a plan first whereas the Resourceful Oranges will jump in by intuitively being able to know where to start, and move forward quickly. The excitement of starting and ending a project fulfills the needs of Organized Golds and Resourceful Oranges.

Where can problems come up

If you think that the world would be an easier place if everyone shared the same dimensions, you'll see that is not the case at all. You need to avoid being too set in your own ways, and see things from the other dimensions' perspective to avoid challenges.

As an Inquiring Green, you can have challenges with other Inquiring Greens. One thing that really bugs you is having your competence challenged or not being given the space to share your ideas. You know that your ideas are well thought out and researched, but another Inquiring Green will also know the same about their ideas. If you dismiss their ideas or they dismiss yours, there is going to be conflict.

As an Organized Gold you can have challenges with other Organized Golds. If you have your idea of a timeline and the way a task should be done and another Organized Gold has a different approach, and neither side sees a need to change there is going to be conflict. Challenges can also come up in situations where family traditions need to merge with others. This can also happen in the workplace when a reorganization occurs and departments or companies merge and find themselves all under one roof. Changes in structure can be challenging for Organized Golds.

As an Authentic Blue you generally have fewer challenges with other Authentic Blues because you value harmony and do your best to avoid conflict. Usually, you will talk things through and find a solution you can both live with. You can have minor communication problems with other Authentic Blues depending on the makeup of their plaid and how Introverted or Extraverted they are.

As a Resourceful Orange, you also have fewer challenges with other Resourceful Oranges because ultimately you just want to move on with things. Life is too short. You will often walk away from potential conflict. You are pretty good at seeing both sides and are happy to agree to disagree. However, if you look at the conflict as a competition, you can be extremely determined. Winning can be very important.

While a lot of similarities can be found between the dimensions, there are some pretty big differences as well. Resourceful Oranges can get impatient when Authentic Blues take too long to make a point. Authentic Blues can feel hurt or frustrated if you think Resourceful Oranges are being insensitive with their off-the-cuff comments. Authentic Blues are very concerned about including others in the decisions making process and like to discuss before acting. Resourceful Oranges like to jump in and get going, and figure things out along the way. So, even though Authentic Blues don't like conflict and Resourceful Oranges would rather move past it, you can, and do have problems with each other at times.

Organized Golds are very concrete, detailed and task-oriented. Inquiring Greens are abstract, big-picture and process-oriented. Inquiring Greens need to have space and freedom to do things their own way. Organized Golds prefer more specific directions. It's easy to see how these differences could create problems between the two of you.

Inquiring Greens like using abstract, conceptual and theoretical terms and want to take time to think and analyze all the information they have gathered before putting things into action. However, Resourceful Oranges have very little patience for semantics and just want to jump in and get things going; you get frustrated by abstraction and delays. There is lots of potential here for both communication and action problems.

Authentic Blues are driven by relationships, so they like to make sure that everyone is heard before a decision is reached.

While Organized Golds are also very concerned about others, you are primarily planners and organizers. So, you want to make a decision, start planning and executing, often at a pace much faster than Authentic Blues might like. Also, don't forget that Organized Golds like to have a detailed plan and timelines where Authentic Blues like things to be more flexible and open-ended. These differences lead to action problems between the two of you.

While Inquiring Greens and Authentic Blues both see the big picture, they have some communication challenges. Inquiring Greens prefer to be objective and direct in their language. Well, without meaning to, Inquiring Greens can hurt Authentic Blue feelings. What you need to realize is that Authentic Blues put a piece of themselves into everything they do, otherwise they wouldn't be doing it. When you criticize their work, you criticize them as a human being.

Authentic Blues need to understand that Inquiring Greens are not cold, unfeeling people. In fact, they feel very deeply. However, they may not be comfortable sharing their feelings and can find it annoying when asked to do so. Equally, they can be frustrated by the Authentic Blues need to soften the blow as they prefer to get to the heart of the matter quickly and prefer objective and direct language.

Organized Golds and Resourceful Oranges have challenges when it comes to action. Organized Golds, like to work on one thing at a time and have a detailed plan, a timeline, and clear instructions on how to do the job. Resourceful Oranges function best when they are multi-tasking, they get excited by doing things at the last minute and like to have the freedom to do things their own way. These opposite ways of doing things can cause a lot of conflict, and it takes compromise on both sides to make things work, but it can absolutely happen.

Understanding and appreciating the differences amongst the four dimensions is the best way for you to live life to its fullest. Sharing the same dimension with someone else is no guarantee that you won't have any challenges. It's important to remember where your similarities are and use them to your collective advantage. When it comes to differences, learning to overcome challenges by compromising will strengthen all types of work and relationships.

You started this journey by filling out a questionnaire, and you've gained some valuable insight while working your way through this book. What was revealed as your most preferred dimension in the questionnaire may or may not be what you think yours really is. Chances are it makes up a big part of your plaid, but that's the thing about Personality, it's not an exact science. There are so many factors in your life that shape who you are. That's why no one is just one dimension... and that's what keeps life interesting!

The numbers on your questionnaire could exactly match someone else's, but you can still be completely different. It's possible to share the same values, needs, and wants, yet at the end of a long day around people, you can be energized, and the other be completely drained. How Extraverted or Introverted you are isn't determined by how shy or outgoing you are, it's all about where you get your energy from. There are definitely joys and challenges about both; understanding what those are helps keep things balanced.

Your needs and values influence every aspect of your life;

personal and work relationships, what you like to do, and how you like to do things. Every dimension has their own unique needs and values, but as you have seen, there is often a lot of overlap. When they have been met, you are fulfilled, happy, and confident; you function better as a human being.

How you communicate with others, and how you want others to communicate with you can be a tricky balance. It's important to shift away from thinking "how do I want to receive this message?" to "how do they want to receive this message?" It doesn't mean you need to completely change your style; you just need to take other ways of communicating into consideration. You don't communicate in a way that is hard for others on purpose; you're doing what comes naturally. Truly understanding what others want and being able to adjust your approach can be difficult, but worth it in the long run.

Our family, friends, co-workers and members of the community all come in and out of our lives at different times. There's good reason why you spend time with the people that you do. If everyone were to think and act the same as each other all the time, life would be pretty boring, and not a lot would get done. In all kinds of relationships, it's important to focus on the strengths that everyone brings, and remember that opposites not only attract, but also bring balance to relationships. Understanding what you and the people you are close with need in a relationship will only strengthen your bond.

Conflict is bound to happen in every area of life. While it's not always possible to prevent it, you can do a lot to resolve it. When you are stressed or out of esteem you tend to lead with your preferred dimension. By understanding how your dimension acts when in conflict, you will be able to use your plaid when it doesn't serve you well. People genuinely don't seek out conflict, but we all have ideas and different things that we feel passionately about. Knowing how the other dimensions act when in conflict helps you decide how to best approach a conflict with them.

How you act at work is an extension of who you are. Your values, natural talents, and needs are all reflected in the work you do. Whether you are a leader or an employee, recognizing your own, unique plaid, as well as that of others will make for a happier, more productive work environment. A workplace made up of all the dimensions, both Introverted and Extraverted uses everyone's strengths and talents to do great things.

Knowing and understanding your own Personality Dimensions is a skill in itself, but fine tuning your Personality Radar and being able to "read" the dimensions will take you even further in life. Being able to shift your approach, be it at work, social situations, or anywhere you are meeting new people allows you to start off on the right foot and create a great rapport. It's not an exact science, especially since you can only go off of how someone is acting. They could be calling on the other colours in their plaid in a given situation, or are playing a role for the situation they are in. You can only look for the clues to tune into what others want and need to find common ground.

Living and working with other dimensions isn't a chore, it's an opportunity. It's a chance to come together to develop a strong bond by recognizing your similarities and appreciating the different gifts that everyone brings with them. When all the dimensions feel valued, seen, and appreciated the resulting harmony can be unstoppable.

Manufactured by Amazon.ca
Bolton, ON